United States
Department
of Agriculture

Forest Service

**Rocky Mountain
Research Station**

Research Paper
RMRS-RP-61CD

April 2007

Development and Evaluation of the Photoload Sampling Technique

Robert E. Keane and Laura J. Dickinson

I0410992

Keane, Robert E.; Dickinson, Laura J. 2007. **Development and evaluation of the photoload sampling technique**. Research Paper RMRS-RP-61CD. Fort Collins, CO: U.S. Department of Agriculture, Forest Service, Rocky Mountain Research Station. 29 p.

Abstract

Wildland fire managers need better estimates of fuel loading so they can accurately predict potential fire behavior and effects of alternative fuel and ecosystem restoration treatments. This report presents the development and evaluation of a new fuel sampling method, called the photoload sampling technique, to quickly and accurately estimate loadings for six common surface fuel components using downward looking and oblique photographs depicting a sequence of graduated fuel loadings of synthetic fuelbeds. This report details the methods used to construct the photoload sequences (series of photos depicting gradually increasing loadings) for the six fuel components. A companion paper (RMRS-GTR-190) presents the set of photoload sequences developed from this study for common fuelbed conditions found in the northern Rocky Mountains of Montana, USA, along with a detailed sampling protocol that can be used with these photoload picture series to estimate fuel component loadings in the field at various levels of effort and scale. An evaluation of the photoload sampling technique was conducted where 29 participants were asked to estimate loadings for the six fuel components on five sites using the photoload technique. These visual estimates were compared with actual measured loadings to obtain estimates of accuracy and precision. We found that photoload estimates consistently underestimated fuel loadings (average bias 0.182 kg m^{-2} or 0.8 tons $acre^{-1}$) but the error of the estimate (0.018 kg m^{-2} or 0.08 tons $acre^{-1}$) was within 10 to 50 percent of the mean depending on fuel component. We also found that accuracy and precision of the photoload estimates increased with increasing field experience and also with increasing fuel loadings.

Keywords: fuel load loading, fuel sampling, photo series, line intersect inventory, wildland fire and fuels

The Authors

Robert E. Keane is a Research Ecologist with the USDA Forest Service, Rocky Mountain Research Station at the Missoula Fire Sciences Laboratory, Missoula, MT. Since 1985, Keane has developed various ecological computer models for the Fire Effects Project for research and management applications. His most recent research includes the synthesis of a First Order Fire Effects Model; construction of mechanistic ecosystem process models that integrate fire behavior and fire effects into succession simulation; restoration of whitebark pine in the Northern Rocky Mountains; spatial simulation of successional communities on the landscape using GIS and satellite imagery; and the mapping of fuels and fire regimes for fire behavior prediction and hazard analysis. He received his B.S. degree in forest engineering in 1978 from the University of Maine, Orono; his M.S. degree in forest ecology from the University of Montana, Missoula, in 1985; and his Ph.D. degree in forest ecology from the University of Idaho, Moscow, in 1994.

Laura J. Dickinson has been a Biological Technician since 2002 with the USDA Forest Service Rocky Mountain Research Station at the Missoula Fire Sciences Laboratory, Missoula, MT. She has contributed to several projects within the Fire Ecology/Fuels Research Project including data collection and analysis for studies on whitebark pine, relict ponderosa pine mortality in the Bob Marshall Wilderness Area, fuels, and fuel sampling techniques. She received her B.S. degree in Aquatic Wildlife Biology in 2003 from the University of Montana, Missoula.

Contents

The use of trade or firm names in this publication is for reader information and does not imply endorsement by the U.S. Department of Agriculture of any product or service

---

Acknowledgments

We thank Wayne Lyngholm, Myron Holland, Curtis Johnson, and Daniel Covington of the Missoula Fire Sciences Laboratory, USDA Forest Service Rocky Mountain Research Station for all their help in the field and in the photography studio. We thank Ian Grob and Jim Kautz at Missoula Technology Development Center, Montana, for the use of their photo studio and equipment and their expertise in taking still photographs. We also thank the people who participated in the evaluation and review of the method: Eva Karau, Alisa Keyser, Kathy Gray, Elizabeth Reinhardt, Ed Matthews, Sharon Hood, Mick Harrington, Melanie Miller, Dennis Simmerman, Richard Hannah, Mitch Dougherty, Matt Reeves, Kori Buford, Colin Hardy, Russ Parsons, Helen Smith of the Rocky Mountain Research Station Missoula Fire Sciences Laboratory; Laura Ward, Steve Slaughter, Matt Galyardt, Brandon Sheehan, and Vick Applegate of the Lolo National Forest; Vicki Edwards of the Clearwater National Forest; and John Caratti and Duncan Lutes, Systems for Environmental Management. We also thank those who provided excellent reviews of the system: Jim Brown and Bill Fischer, retired USDA Forest Service scientists; Duncan Lutes, Systems for Environmental Management; Roger Ottmar and Clint Wright, USDA Forest Service, Pacific Northwest Research Station, FERA Group; and Curtis Johnson and Rudy King, USDA Forest Service Rocky Mountain Research Station.

Development and Evaluation of the Photoload Sampling Technique

Robert E. Keane and Laura J. Dickinson

Introduction

Wildland fire managers need better estimates of fuel loadings in forest and rangeland ecosystems of the United States so they can more accurately predict the fire behavior and effects of alternative fuel and ecosystem restoration treatments using sophisticated computer models (Laverty and Williams 2000; GAO 2003, 2004). Fuel loadings, along with fuel moisture, are the most important factors that fire managers can control for implementing prescribed burn treatments (Agee 1993; DeBano and others 1998). High fuel loadings usually result in high fire intensities, deep soil heating, abundant smoke generation, and high plant mortality (Reinhardt and others 1997). An accurate estimation of fuel loading will allow managers to more accurately estimate effects of fire treatments using models such as FOFEM and CONSUME (Ottmar and others 1993; www.fs.fed.us/nw/fera/consume.html; Reinhardt and Keane 1998; www.frames.gov). These models can then be used to plan, prioritize, design, and implement important fuel treatments for restoring historical fire regimes and reducing hazardous fuels to save lives and property (Mutch 1994; Laverty and Williams 2000).

The research presented here is a comprehensive effort to develop a sampling method, called the *photoload sampling technique,* that quickly and accurately estimates surface fuel component loadings using visual assessments of loading referencing a sequence of downward looking photographs depicting graduated fuel loadings by fuel component. This report will first detail the methods used to construct the photoload sequences so that this procedure can be repeated elsewhere for other fuel types. The developed photoload sequences are published in a companion document (Keane and Dickinson 2007; RMRS-GTR-190) along with a detailed sampling protocol for using these picture sequences in the field. We evaluated this new sampling method by comparing the photoload estimates of fuel loading as estimated by 29 participants in a field study with the fuel loadings actually sampled on 1 m^2 microplots and at the 2,500 m^2 macroplot level.

Fuel loading is defined in this study as the mass of a fuel component per unit horizontal area, expressed in this report with the units kg m^{-2} or tons acre^{-1}. Fuel loadings are usually stratified into several unique components specifically designed for predicting fire behavior and effects (Fosberg 1970). First, fuels are stratified by canopy and surface fuels where canopy fuels are usually, but not always, defined as aerial biomass 2 meters (6 feet) above the ground. Surface fuels are those fuels that support the propagation of a surface fire (Rothermel 1972; Albini 1976; van Wagner 1977). This report only deals with surface fuels. Downed dead woody surface fuels are usually separated into four or five size classes based on the diameter of the woody fuel particle (Fosberg 1970; Burgan and Rothermel 1984). Other surface fuel components include live and dead shrubs and herbaceous vegetation, litter, and duff. This study did not create photos of litter and duff fuelbeds so loadings of these fuel components must be measured with conventional techniques.

Background

Challenges sampling surface fuels—Accurately measuring surface fuel loadings in the field is difficult because it requires a complex integration of several sampling methods that were designed for implementation at disparate scales. Downed dead woody fuels are typically sampled using line intersect techniques introduced by van Wagner (1968) and improved as the planar intersect techniques by Brown (1970, 1971, 1974) and subsequently implemented into many surface fuel inventory sampling systems such as FIREMON (www.fire.org/firemon) (Lutes and others 2006). Planar intersect techniques were designed for estimating downed woody fuel loadings at the stand level using linear transects that define sampling planes. Dead and live shrub and herbaceous fuels are often measured using time-consuming destructive methods that involve clipping all fuels within small microplots or estimated from indirect techniques such as calculating loadings from canopy cover and height estimates using bulk densities and allometric equations. Loadings of duff are often calculated as the product of depths and bulk densities measured at various points along the fuel transects. Litter is usually measured by collecting and weighing a subsample of plots (Brown and others 1982). Many times, the scale and error of surface fuel measurements are incompatible and inconsistent across the fuel components. Log loading, for example, often varies at much greater spatial scales than fine fuel loading because of the large size of the logs. These methods, individually or collectively, are also rather time-consuming and require training and field expertise. What is needed is an inexpensive, easy, and quick fuel sampling technique that can provide consistent estimates of fuel loadings at the level of accuracy required by the fire behavior and effects models for fuel treatment planning. These fuel loading estimates must be able to be used as inputs to fire behavior and effects models, and they must measure fuel components at the appropriate spatial scale.

Many factors contribute to the difficulty of sampling surface fuel loadings. First, there are many types of wildland fuels and the set of distinct components needed to describe these fuels is often dictated by the objective of the fuel sampling project (Sandberg and others 2001). For example, a description of fuels for fire behavior prediction requires the downed dead woody surface fuel loadings to be stratified by type and particle size classes that are related to their rate of drying and time to ignition (Fosberg 1970). Other stratifications can be dead or live, woody or non-woody, and surface or canopy (Burgan 1987). Another reason fuel sampling is difficult is that fuels have high spatial and temporal variability and that variability and its inherent scale is often different for each fuel component. Log loadings, for example, tend to be more variable across fine spatial scales (1-10 meters, 3-30 feet) than twig and branch loadings because of their large diameter and length. Log loadings may be more variable across finer time scales because sudden disturbance events usually cause treefall in many forest stands (Harmon and others 1986).

The diversity and variability of wildland surface fuels often precludes a standardized measurement protocol that is appropriate for all fuel components because of the above mentioned scale issues. It is difficult to sample all fuels using only one technique or method because of the size, frequency, and position of the fuel components. For example, fixed microplots would be efficient for sampling duff, litter, and small woody particles, but somewhat inefficient for large logs and canopy fuels. Therefore, operational fuel sampling has always included a diverse set of integrated fuel sampling methods (Brown and others 1982; Lutes and others 2006). Field sampling times often increase as more fuel components are included in the sampling protocol. For example, live and dead shrubby and herbaceous fuels can be measured along the planar intersect transects, but it takes time to clip and weigh the material or visually assess loading from estimates of plant height and cover. What is needed is a sampling method that uses the same protocols to estimate loadings for each component. These protocols must also have the ability to estimate fuel loading at the appropriate scale of variability for each component.

Many agencies use a combination of approaches and methods applied at a local level to estimate fuel loadings resulting in datasets that are often incomplete and incomparable across regions or ecosystems (Lutes and others 2006). Few land management agencies have the funding for standardized, comprehensive fuel sampling programs to conduct accurate and consistent fuel inventories. And, many field crews do not possess the training and expertise required to generate high quality fuels data. A fuel sampling method that is quickly taught and easily used by field crews would greatly benefit fire management because, in some cases, fire crews could be inventorying critical wildland fuels when they are not needed for fire fighting.

Current sampling methods—There appear to be five general methods for sampling fuels. *Fixed plot methods* are those that use a plot frame of a fixed area to delineate a sampling area. All fuels within that area are collected, dried, and weighed to determine loadings (mass per unit area) (Harmon and others 1986; Harmon and Sexton 1996). This includes those techniques that use large circular or square plots along with those that use a strip plot layout. The advantage of this method is that fuel components (woody, litter, duff, and so on) can be collected using the same plot frame or nested plot frames of varying sizes to accurately estimate variability at the appropriate scale. This is often the most accurate method of sampling fuels. The disadvantage is that the collection and weighing of material on the fixed plot is time and cost intensive and therefore the method is used mostly for research efforts and rarely for operational fuel inventories. It is also difficult to determine the number of fixed plots to adequately capture the variability of different fuel components within the sample unit (stand, polygon, landscape) because the fuels are highly variable in space and time and are often clumped in "jackpots."

Planar intercept methods are the most common sampling techniques for sampling downed woody fuels for inventory projects (van Wagner 1968). This involves counting woody fuel particles or measuring their diameters as they intercept a vertical sampling plane that is of a fixed length and height (Brown 1970, 1974). These intercepts can then be converted to loadings using standard formulae. The advantage of this method is that it is easy to use and can sometimes be scaled to match the sampling unit and fuel conditions by altering the dimensions of the sampling plane. The method can be taught to novice field technicians and subsequent results are moderately repeatable. However, this method only pertains to downed dead woody particles and may require a large number of sampling transects (bottom of sampling plane) under heavy and highly variable fuel conditions (Lutes and others 2006). And, the scale for realistically describing fine fuel loadings (m^2) of all components is not possible with planar intercept because logs tend to vary at much coarser scales.

Recent research has found that *angle gauge methods* are effective at measuring loadings of coarse woody debris (Gove and others 1999; Gove and others 2001). Here, an angle gauge is used in a point sampling strategy to identify logs that should be sampled. This method is quick and effective but only is used for coarse woody debris (large logs) and has limited use for fuel inventories that require loadings of fine fuels for fire behavior predictions. It was not used in this study.

An often-used, fast, and easy fuel sampling technique is the *photo series method*. In this method, a person walks into the sampling unit (plot, stand, or landscape) and visually matches the observed conditions by fuelbed category with one or more photographs from a set of oblique pictures characterizing common vegetation types and site conditions (Fischer 1981; Ottmar and others 2004). This method is used by many fire management agencies to get a quick estimate of fuel loadings. It is easily taught and the photos are easily created. However, this technique can be inaccurate for fine fuels and is often not repeatable (Lutes 1999, 2002). The photograph series may not adequately capture the fuelbed conditions needed to estimate loadings of all fuel components at the appropriate scale. Sometimes, the fine fuel components (1, 10, 100 hour downed woody) are not visible within these pictures so this technique may be ineffective for predicting fire behavior based on fuels inventories.

The last fuel sampling strategy, called the *fuel model method,* is perhaps the easiest and quickest, but it also may be the least accurate and repeatable. A fuel model is a set of loadings for a discrete set of fuel components that describes some biophysical setting (Sandberg and others 2001). Sometimes, fuel models are categories of a classification of fuel loadings (Lutes and others [in prep]) and sometimes fuel models are created by summarizing fuel loadings for categories of vegetation-based classifications (Reinhardt and others 1997; Sandberg and others 2001). Fuel models can also be linked to specific vegetation, site, and stand history characteristics (Keane and others 2001) so that a field person could key the fuel model from conditions observed within the sampling unit. This technique is quite useful in fuel mapping efforts, especially those using remotely sensed imagery, because it provides a means for extrapolating sampled fuels across the landscape based on the keyed characteristics. However, this method is often inaccurate for fine scale fuel inventories because, like the photos in the photo series method, fuel models are oversimplifications of actual fuel conditions and fuel components are spatially independent and highly clustered.

What is needed is a fuel sampling technique that accurately and consistently measures loadings across a wide variety of components. In addition, this technique must be 1) easily taught to field crews, 2) quickly implemented in the field, 3) scalable so that any sampling unit can be measured and the fuel components are measured at the appropriate spatial scale, 4) accurate enough so that estimates can be used as input to fire models, and 5) repeatable so that estimates can be measured at a precision that is required by fire management applications. We designed the photoload sampling technique to satisfy these design requirements. The photoload technique is not intended to replace the previously discussed protocols and methods. Rather, it is intended to be a viable alternative when the objectives of the sampling effort and the resources available to perform the sampling match the design characteristics of the photoload technique. For example, a fire management agency might require the accurate estimation of fuel loads but their field crews have limited experience in planar intersect fuel sampling and there may be little funding available for training; therefore, the photoload technique may be a viable option.

Study Objectives

This study had four distinct objectives that were linked together to ultimately deliver a method of estimating surface fuels using the photoload technique. These objectives were:

- *Develop methods for producing photoload sequences (downward-looking photographs of synthetic fuel-beds depicting graduated loadings).*
- *Develop a set of photoload sequences for use in the northern Rocky Mountains for estimating fuel loadings of six major fuel components using photos of synthetic fuelbeds.*
- *Evaluate this technique by comparing estimates from a number of people with conditions actually measured on the ground.*

- *Develop a sampling protocol for estimating fuel loadings using the photoload sequences.*

The methods for producing the photoload sequences (photoload development methods) reported here are sufficiently detailed so others can repeat this effort and create new photoload sequences for other fuel types such as masticated fuels. The photoload sequences developed for this study were for the northern Rocky Mountains with the shrub and herbaceous components described by only 11 species. However, we feel these pictures are sufficiently robust to sample shrub and herb loadings for many but not all stand conditions in the region (see companion report Keane and Dickinson 2007; RMRS-GTR-190 for these sequences). The photoload sampling procedure was designed to allow the user to sample fuels at a point, plot, and stand level so that the variability of fuel components can be captured at the appropriate spatial scale. The photoload sampling technique was designed for fire managers and researchers to monitor and inventory fuels, and the evaluators in this study reflect that audience (these protocols are also detailed in the companion report). And last, the photoload fuel loadings estimated from the field evaluation are compared to actual fuel loadings measured on the ground to provide an estimate of the precision and accuracy of the photoload sampling method.

Methods

This section is organized by the four study objectives and is written with sufficient detail so others can replicate these procedures to produce photoload loading sequences for other fuel components or fuel types. First, the procedures used to create the photoload sequences are discussed and then the procedures used to test, evaluate, and refine the photoload technique are presented.

We selected the following six fuel components to be included in the photoload technique:

- 1 hour – <1 cm (0.25 inch) diameter downed, dead, woody fuels
- 10 hour – 1-2.5 cm (0.25-1.0 inch) diameter downed, dead, woody fuels
- 100 hour – 2.5-7 cm (1-3 inch) diameter downed, dead, woody fuels
- 1000 hour (logs) – >7 cm (3+ inch) diameter downed, dead, woody fuels
- Shrub – Dead and live shrubby fuels
- Herbaceous – Dead and live grass and forb fuels

These components were selected because they are required as inputs in many fire behavior and effects models, and they are the most common components found in the northern Rocky Mountains of Montana, USA. Duff and litter were not included in this study because their loadings are highly dependent on depth of the layer above mineral soil and this depth is difficult to detect or estimate with downward looking photographs. Future versions of photoload will have methods for estimating these important ground fuels. Canopy fuels were not included because a useful photoguide has already been created by Scott and Reinhardt (2005).

The photoload sampling technique is composed of two separate elements. The first element is the photoload sequences consisting of digital photographs of fuelbeds with gradually increasing loadings for each of the six fuel components. The second element is the set of procedures that reference the photoload sequences to estimate loadings by fuel component called the "photoload sampling protocol." Both are detailed in the companion document RMRS-GTR-190 (Keane and Dickinson 2007).

Developing the Photoload Sequences

In short, development of the photoload sequences involved 1) collecting the fuels to be photographed in the field and bringing them back to the laboratory to measure dry weights and densities, 2) constructing the fuelbeds in sequential series of increasing fuel loads for each component, 3) photographing these fuels on a stage in a studio, and 4) importing the digital photographs into software to create the photoload sequences.

We use the term "fuelbed" to describe the fuels within a fixed area. This area is typically 1 m^2 for all fuels except for logs (greater than 7 cm or 3 inches in diameter). The fuel on the fuelbed has a predetermined weight and once that fuel is put within the fixed area that weight gives the fuelbed a loading (mass per unit area). Fine woody fuels are the 1, 10, and 100 hour downed dead woody fuel components. Shrub and herbaceous fuels are photographed as live specimens but pictures are used to estimate dead fuel loads because we measured only dry weighs for photographed fuel loadings. Logs are considered 1000 hour dead downed woody fuel in this study.

Collecting fuel to photograph—For the fine woody fuel, we collected approximately 10.0 kg (22 lbs) of 1, 10, and 100 hour fuels from forests surrounding Missoula, MT, USA. These samples were collected from a variety of habitat types and vegetation communities to capture the full range of wood from various tree species in the area. The collected samples were dried in an oven at 80° C for three days. We then created sets of fuels that were of various weights to facilitate the creation of the fuelbeds to be photographed. These sets were collections of fuels that weighed exactly 0.01, 0.1, 0.5, and 1.0 kg that were stored in containers so that they were easily accessible when we created the fuelbeds to photograph. Weights of some of the larger wood (100 hour fuels) were written directly on the particle to help in fuelbed construction.

We decided to take a different approach in photographing large woody fuel (1000 hour logs) for a number of reasons. First, logs are heavy so they are unwieldy and difficult to work within the confined conditions of a studio. It is often difficult to determine the dry weight of large logs because most do not fit into the oven, so sub-sampling is necessary and this may contribute to unacceptable error. The variability of log density, because of rot, bark, and species differences, also makes it difficult to consistently construct fuelbeds of known loadings. And, it is difficult to control the characteristics of the log fuelbed because real logs are often crooked, tapered, cracked, or split. So, instead of collecting actual log material, we purchased lengths of 6 and 10 inch (15 cm and 25 cm) diameter cardboard tubing from the local hardware store and painted the tubes brown to mimic logs. Cardboard tubes were selected because they are light and easy to handle. We bought two sizes (6 inch and 10 inch diameters) to match the common diameters observed in the field (Brown and See 1981; Brown and Bevins 1986). After numerous trials and photography sessions, we felt that the photographs of the brown tube closely resembled real logs from a distance. Log loadings were computed by multiplying the volume of the tube logs by the specific weight of real wood. We used the density of Douglas-fir (480 kg m^{-3} from Wenger 1984) for this study but could have used other densities to more accurately fit our region or species. We then cut the tubes in different lengths to allow the construction of a variety of fuelbeds that represented known loadings.

Collecting shrub and herbaceous plant material to photograph was significantly more complex than the collection of woody fuels because the plant specimens needed to portray typical conditions observed on the ground. We decided to only photograph live shrub and live herbaceous fuelbeds because live fuels are easier to work with and since the loadings are based on dry weight, the live loadings would be identical for dead shrub and herbs. However, we found that it was difficult to build live fuelbeds of a known loading because of the high and variable moisture contents. We could not dry the live fuel first because the dried material would be shriveled for our photographs. Moreover, in our first attempts at photographing live plant fuelbeds, we found

that the collected shrub and herbaceous material dried and shriveled significantly during the photography sessions and the resultant photographs of semi-cured material did not depict commonly observed conditions in forested communities. Therefore, we decided to integrate the collection and photography process into a two-day sampling procedure. On the first day, we collected samples of herbaceous and shrub species in the forests near Missoula, MT, and used these samples to calculate the moisture content of the plants as they occurred in the field. We weighed, dried overnight, and re-weighed the collected material the next morning to obtain the moisture content. On the second day, we collected a larger live fuel sample that was used to create the fuelbeds to photograph. We calculated fuelbed loadings by adjusting the live weight of the material collected on the second day to a dry weight basis using the moisture contents computed that morning from the material collected on the first day. This allowed us to create live fuelbeds of specific dry-weight loadings and also to photograph live plant fuelbeds that are similar to those observed in the field.

Shrub fuelbed construction presented yet another problem in describing loading for the photoload sequences. Since shrubs are composed of woody material and foliage, it is sometimes necessary to stratify shrub fuel loadings by live woody fuel size classes and foliage for fire modeling. However, it is unrealistic to portray the shrub live fuel loadings by these components using the photoload sequences because the resultant photographs would not depict actual conditions observed on the ground. Moreover, shrub morphology differs by species, age, canopy position, and disturbance history (browsing and fire) so it is difficult to take pictures that would consistently quantify shrub loadings by the live fuel components. We finally decided to portray shrub fuelbeds in the photoload sequences using upright intact live shrub cuttings, but, when we weighed the shrubs, we decided to separate shrub fuels into woody and foliage and derived a proportion of shrub fuel by live fuel component.

We calculated the density (kg m^{-3}) of each downed dead woody fuel component because recent research has shown there are significant differences in wood density by the species, rot class, and size class (Van Wagtendonk and others 1996). The measured density estimates allowed us to compare our photographed loadings with loadings measured in the field during the evaluation procedure mentioned later and also to compare our results with results from other studies. We took 25 samples of each of the four woody fuel components (1, 10, 100, and 1000 hr) including logs from the same areas where we collected the fine woody fuels and live fuels to photograph for the study. These samples were approximately 20 to 30 cm long. We measured the diameters at each end of the particle, and the length of the particle, to calculate volume. Then, we dried the samples at 80 °C for three days and weighed them. The density was calculated by dividing the dry weight by the volume of the particle. Usually, density is measured as a specific gravity by placing the particle in a Kraus Jolly specific gravity balance and measuring the displaced liquid (Van Wagtendonk and others 1996) but we did not have access to this apparatus.

Photographing the fuelbeds—This task involved photographing fuelbeds of increasing fuel loadings by fuel component with a digital camera. The photographs were designed to be used as reference for the visual estimation of fuel loadings on the ground. It took several weeks and many trials to determine the best set-up to take high resolution, high quality digital photographs that could be used for estimating loadings. First, we tried taking fuelbed photographs outside in a parking lot but light conditions were too variable. Then, we constructed an apparatus inside a large warehouse to take the photos but found significant shadowing in many of the pictures because of inadequate lighting. We could have corrected the lighting problems but found an indoor studio at the Missoula Technology Development Center (MTDC) that perfectly fit our needs (fig. 1).

All pictures were taken with a Nikon D100 digital camera at 3008x2000 pixel resolution with automatic exposure using center-weighted meter settings and a sensitivity of ISO 320. Digital pictures were stored as TIFF-RGR (8-bit) files. Many digital cameras have adequate resolution to take the photoload pictures. All photos were checked for clarity and sharpness on a monitor after the photo was taken. Using Nikon View Software, we were able to thoroughly document each digital photo with photographic and fuelbed details in a header file. We also wrote the date, person, photo number, fuel component and species for shrub and herbaceous fuels, and loading on a dry erase board adjacent to the photographed fuelbed and visible in the uncropped picture for future reference. We also recorded the average height of shrubs and herbs.

a

b

c

Figure 1—Design of the apparatus used to take the downward looking photographs for the photoload sequences: a) the camera is set on a step ladder and hooked to three flashes surrounding the fuelbed, b) the fuelbed is placed directly below the camera, c) the photographed fuelbed that is then cropped at the tape lines for a 1 meter by 1 meter photo.

The point of view was perhaps the most important factor in the design of the fuelbed photography. Conventional photo series photographs have an eye-level point of view with an oblique view angle looking nearly parallel with the ground (Fischer 1981). This provides a good view of conditions at the stand level, but many fuel components, especially fine woody and herbaceous fuels, may be obstructed because of the oblique angle and blocking plants, or fuels may be indistinguishable due to the long distance to the fuelbed. We decided to design our photography to emphasize differences in loadings within a fuel component. Therefore, pictures of fine woody fuels were taken looking directly downward with a field of view and view point that approximates that seen at eye level by a person in the field (figs. 1a and 1b). Since logs vary at coarser scales, we photographed them at eye level looking at approximately the same oblique angle as in the photo series. However, we removed all obstructions so that the differences between loadings were easily detected.

Building fine woody fuelbeds and taking photoload pictures—The easiest fuelbeds to create and photograph were the fine woody fuels (1, 10, and 100 hour woody particles). The small size of the fuel particles coupled with the characteristic that these fuels tend to align along two dimensions (depth is not important in many circumstances) meant that we only needed to take overhead photographs to adequately portray fuel loadings. A thin, white, 2 by 2 m (6.5 x 6.5 foot) sheet of plastic material painted with white opaque spray paint (to prevent glare) was placed on the floor of the studio (fig. 1). A boundary slightly larger than the 1 m^2 square was taped with blue masking tape onto the white surface so that after the photo was taken it could be digitally cropped inside the boundary to create an image of exactly one square meter (figs. 1b and 1c). A camera was mounted on a ladder approximately 3 meters (10 feet) above the fuel bed. Several flashes were attached to the camera and placed on all four sides of the white painted square to minimize shadows (fig. 1a). The focal length of the camera's zoom lens was set so that it looked like the picture was taken at eye level. We experimented with various aperture settings and lens speeds but found that the camera's automatic setting worked as well as any setting and seemed the simplest to perform.

Fine woody fuelbeds were created using a process that involved placing fuels of known dry weight on the painted sheet to achieve a desired loading. The fuels were evenly distributed across the one square meter (10 square feet) taped portion of the sheet. We made sure that the fine fuels did not overlay or intersect each other in light loading fuelbeds to minimize shadowing. We created many fuelbeds for each fine woody component from 0.01 kg m^{-2} to 5.0 kg m^{-2} in 0.01 kg m^{-2} increments to 1.0 kg m^{-2} and 0.1 kg m^{-2} increments thereafter. We photographed a number of loadings knowing that the photoload series need not contain all the loading pictures. We used the metric units of kg m^{-2} because it seemed to best fit the scale of the photography and the scale of fuel load spatial distribution for nearly all fuel components.

We tried to represent the entire range of fuel loadings occurring in the field in the photoload sequences. To accomplish this, we analyzed a fuel load database compiled by Lutes and others (2007 [in prep]), as well as the data from various photo series (Fischer 1981), to determine the minimum and maximum loading for each fuel component. We decided to use the 90th percentile maximum and minimum loadings for each fuel component as a guide for limiting the set of photoload pictures. We also decided to include photos with very high loadings to represent slashed stands.

Building and photographing log fuelbeds—Creation of the log photoload sequences presented some significant problems in this study. The spatial scale of log distributions in a stand is somewhat coarser than the 1 m^2 frames used for the other fuel components in this study. Logs can be long and of large diameter so pictures taken at small scales do not adequately portray log loadings, especially for the purpose of visual estimation. We staged pictures of the log fuelbeds outside on a lawn rather than in a studio to accommodate the large scale needed to realistically represent log conditions found in the field. These pictures were taken on a freshly cut grass lawn because the contrast between logs and lawn was greater than the contrast observed when pictures were taken on asphalt, sand, or gravel.

The log fuelbed area was defined by a 100 m^2 trapezoid that matched the view seen through the camera lens (fig. 2). The trapezoid was delineated by a yellow rope to clearly define the boundary in the photos. We chose a 100 m^2 trapezoid because it simplified the process of determining log loading and it best fit the scale of the photography (field of view) and log size distribution. A person stood to the side of the trapezoid with a 6 foot (2 meter) rod for scale in the photos. Logs were uniformly placed flat on the ground throughout the trapezoid unless high loadings required logs to cross each other. A camera was placed on a tripod at 1.6 meters (5 feet) off the ground at approximately 5 meters (16 feet) from the narrow end of the trapezoid. We calculated the total length of cardboard tubing needed to achieve a target loading and photographed gradually increasing loadings from 0.1 to 50 kg m^{-2} to create the photoload sequence. We took two

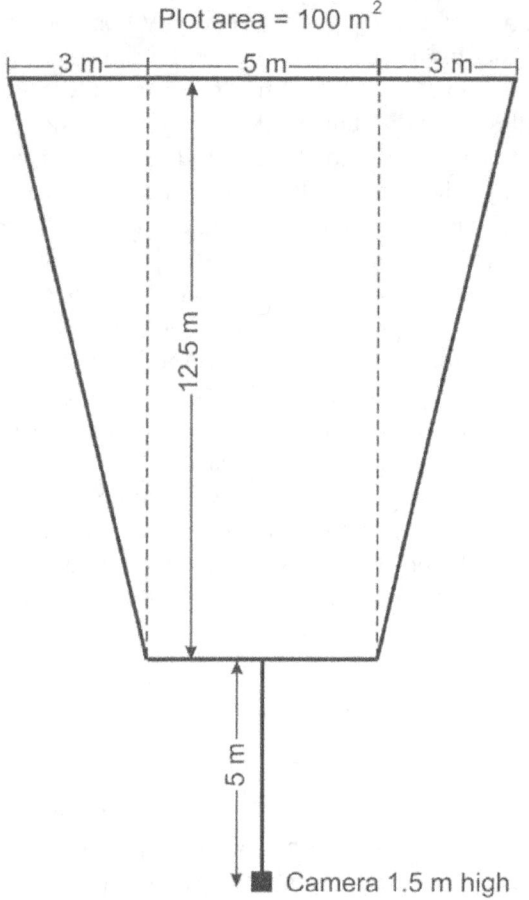

Plot area = 100 m^2

|← 3 m →|← 5 m →|← 3 m →|

12.5 m

5 m

Camera 1.5 m high

Figure 2—The plot trapezoid and corresponding dimensions used to define the area to place the logs to achieve the sequence of loadings for photoload pictures.

series of loading photos—one with the 6 inch diameter tubes and one with the 10 inch diameter tubes.

It became evident as we created the log fuelbeds that log loading could quickly be calculated in the field by knowing the length and average diameter of logs on the plot assuming a standard wood density. Therefore, we decided to augment the photographic photoload sampling technique with a tabular approach where the length and diameter of logs in a 100 m^2 plot are used to estimate loading. We built a series of tables that provided loadings for various log diameters and lengths to use in the field in addition to the photoload photos to estimate loading (see companion document Keane and Dickinson 2007; RMRS-GTR-190). These tables can be used to directly estimate loadings or to check photoload estimates. They can be easily modified to account for different wood density conditions caused by differences in species and decay.

Creating shrub and herb fuelbeds and pictures—We created a fuel platform using methods similar to those of Burgan and Rothermel (1984) that consisted of framed hardware cloth with approximately 1.0 cm wide screen grid (holes) (fig. 3). The frame was slightly larger than one square meter so the image could be digitally cropped to exactly one square meter. Herbaceous and shrubby fuel were threaded through the screen and evenly distributed throughout the entire fuel platform to achieve a fuelbed that looked similar to rooted and upright live plants as they occurred in nature. We placed a familiar object such

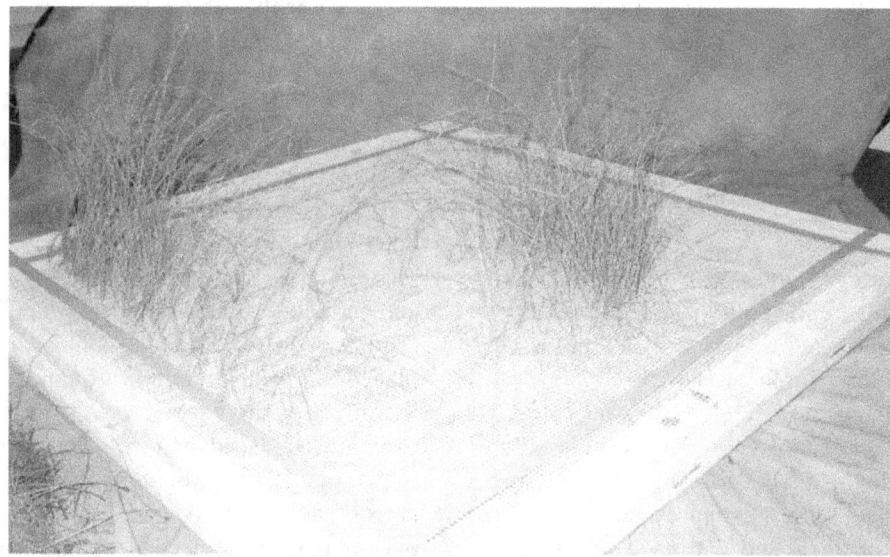

Figure 3—The shrub and herbaceous fuel platform used to arrange the plants so that they resembled conditions observed in the field.

as a hard hat to the side of the shot in the shrub and herb photos and a person with a 6 foot rod in log pictures to help calibrate the user's eye and to provide reference for the average height of the plants in the photos.

Since height is important to shrub and herbaceous loading, both downward looking and oblique photos were taken for the shrub and forb fuel components. The overhead photos were taken with the same specifications as the fine woody fuel photos mentioned above. The oblique photos were taken with a camera mounted on a tripod set five feet high (eye level, 1.5 meters) from a side angle. The same consecutive fuelbed loadings were used for both overhead and oblique photos. We did not have the extensive data set to determine the range of fuelbed loadings for shrubs and herbs, so we chose the range of loadings to best represent a visible change in plant material. Photos ranged from single stems to completely full fuel beds in a series of up to 25 photos.

The fuel platform used to hold plants had some design flaws that demanded a second loading adjustment. The portion of the stem pushed through the hardware cloth screen could not be seen in the digital photos even though we were including this hidden weight in the predetermined loading. To resolve this problem, a sub-sample of each species with a known weight was placed through the screen. The proportion above the screen was then cut, eliminating the portion of stems below the screen that was obscured in the photos. The portion of plants above the screen was then reweighed and used to calculate the proportion of total weight above the screen that was then used, along with moisture content, to adjust the amount of material to thread through the platform screen to achieve the target loading. For example, if the target loading was 10.0 g, and 5.0 percent of the photographed fuel was under the screen and the fuel had a moisture content of 110 percent, then we put 22.05 g (10.0, x 1.05 x 2.1) in the platform.

We decided to use only one species of shrub or herb in a set of photoload sequences for consistency. This presented a major problem for fuel sampling since natural fuelbeds can consist of many species in common forest and rangeland settings. We decided that we would take separate photoload sequences for the most widespread species of shrubs and herbs found in western Montana. Obviously, these species are often mixed in natural settings, but we developed ways to adjust for this mixed situation in the sampling protocol detailed in the companion document (Keane and Dickinson 2007; RMRS-GTR-190). In the end, we took photoload sequences of seven shrub species and four herbaceous species (two grass species and two forb species).

Creating the digital photoload sequences—All digital photographs were downloaded to a computer and stored as files in an organized directory structure. The downloaded digital files were immediately renamed to more intuitive labels using a file-naming convention that included the fuel component and loading in the name. For example, shrub fuelbeds with 1.0 kg m^{-2} loading were named shrub1-00.jpeg. All files were visually checked for errors or abnormalities and if any problems were found, these pictures were taken again. Many of these photos are included on this CD in the directory/pictures.

A template was designed to standardize the arrangement of the digital photographs to be printed on paper so that they could be brought to the field. We used several software packages in this design process (mostly Adobe Photoshop®, CorelDraw®, and Microsoft Photo®). The design included a label at the top of each photo that detailed the loading in both metric (kg m^{-2}) and English (tons acre^{-1}) units. To determine how many photos to include on a page, we printed several sets with 5 to 12 photos per page and had local field personnel decide which set was best for estimating fuel loading. We then realized it was inefficient to include photographs of all loadings because some differences between sequential fuel loading photographs were barely distinguishable in many series, especially for downed dead woody fuels. Therefore, we constructed the photoload series to emphasize differences in fuel loadings rather than present the photoload pictures in finite loading intervals. Once finished, we compiled a bound notebook of the photoload sequences by fuel component on waterproof paper and called this the "photoload reference book" for use in the field during testing and evaluation. During preliminary testing it became evident that there were some design flaws and mistakes in the reference book—some sequences inadequately captured the range of observed conditions. We fixed these flaws and created a final photoload reference book.

Evaluating the Photoload Sampling Technique

Selecting the sites and establishing the plots—We evaluated the photoload technique on five sites on the Ninemile District of the Lolo National Forest in western Montana, USA (Latitude 47 degrees 5 minutes, Longitude 114 degrees 12 minutes) (table 1). These sites were selected to represent common stand types and fuel conditions in the northern Rocky Mountains. Each site had at least five of the six fuel components (table 1), was somewhat flat (less than 10 percent slope), and contained no biophysical abnormalities. Only five sites were selected

Table 1—Characteristics of the five sites used to test and evaluate the photoload sampling technique. Fuel loadings for the 1 hr, 10 hr, 100 hr, shrub, and herbaceous loadings are averages across 25, 1 m^2 microplots using destructive methods of collection, drying, and weighing the fuels. Log loadings are averages of log volume and density measurements on 25, 100 m^2 subplots.

	Site 1	Site 2	Site 3	Site 4	Site 5
Site name	Cayuse 1 (C1)	Cayuse 2 (C2)	Sawmill (S3)	Kries (K4)	Moncure (M5)
Forest cover type	*Pinus ponderosa*	*Pinus ponderosa*	*Pinus ponderosa*	*Pinus ponderosa*	*Larix occidentalis*
Understory cover type	*Festuca scabrella*	*Balsamorhiza sagittata*	*Calamagrostic rubescens*	*Calamagrostic rubescens*	*Berberis repens*
Total tree cover (%)	30	40	30	40	30
Total shrub cover (%)	1	1	20	50	10
Total graminoid cover (%)	50	30	70	70	20
Natural/activity fuel	natural	activity	activity	natural	activity
Fire Behavior Fuel model[1]	2	10	11	5	12
Fuelbed type	grass	light slash	moderate slash	shrub	heavy slash
1 hour loading (kg m^{-2})	0.002	0.001	0.115	0.011	0.260
10 hour loading (kg m^{-2})	0.171	0.130	0.439	0.071	0.557
100 hour loading (kg m^{-2})	0.052	0.070	0.568	0.111	0.785
1000 hour loading (logs) (kg m^{-2})	0.250	0.356	0.403	0.581	3.483
Shrub loading (kg m^{-2})	<0.0001	<0.0001	0.012	0.075	0.008
Herbaceous loading (kg m^{-2})	0.053	0.066	0.062	0.058	0.064
Number of evaluation participants	5	10	14	11	8

[1]The Fire Behavior Fuel Model was estimated from Anderson and others (1982).

because the sampling of reference fuel loadings was difficult and costly, requiring the collection and weighing of fuels within a plot. Another study that compared five fuel sampling techniques was also implemented on these sites (Sikkink and Keane 2008 [in press]).

We used a set of nested plots to test the photoload sampling technique and also to collect actual loadings to evaluate the accuracy and consistency of the photoload method (fig. 4). Sikkink and Keane (2007 [in press]) also used these nested plots to implement sampling protocols of other commonly used fuel sampling techniques for comparison purposes. First, we selected a large topographically homogeneous area within each site and established a 50 meter by 50 meter (2,500 m^2) macroplot. The square macroplot was oriented in the cardinal directions and was clearly marked using bright yellow rope pulled tight at each corner identified by permanent iron bars driven at least 2 feet in the ground. We then divided the macroplot into 25, 10 meter by 10 meter (100 m^2) subplots by stretching rope transects at the 10, 20, 30, and 40 meter marks across the north-to-south and east-to-west directions (fig. 4) and attaching these rope transects to 10 inch nails temporarily driven into the ground. A portable 1 m^2 quadrat (1 meter by 1 meter) made of inch (2.5 cm) diameter plastic PVC pipe was placed in the northeast corner of each subplot to create 25 microplots (fig. 4). Our evaluators estimated and we later measured loadings of logs in the 100 m^2 subplots and loadings of all other fuel components in the 1 m^2 microplots.

Testing and evaluating the photoload technique—We next developed a standardized sampling protocol for people to follow when evaluating the photoload technique so that we could be reasonably assured that consistent methods were used to generate the photoload estimates. We also developed a plot sheet that provided guidance and contained fields for entry of estimated fuel loads. These procedures were recorded in a notebook and taught to all our evaluation participants. These evaluation procedures formed the first attempt at designing a general sampling protocol for the finalized photoload technique (Keane and Dickinson 2007; RMRS-GTR-190).

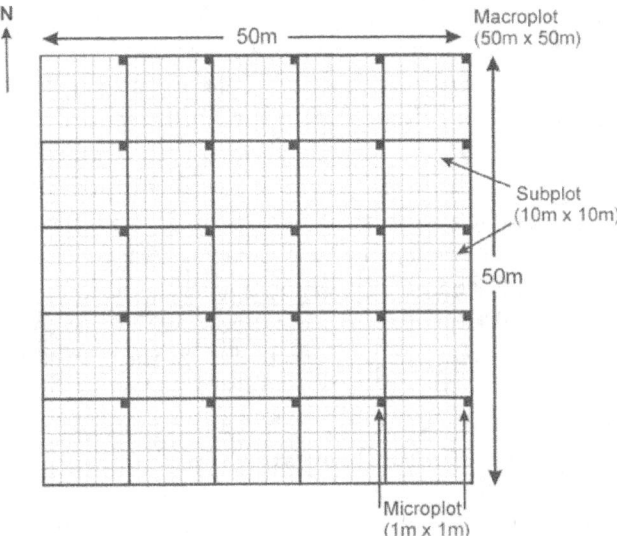

Figure 4—Design and layout of the photoload plot for sampling reference conditions. This plot design was used to nest other plot sampling procedures.

To evaluate the accuracy, precision, and consistency of the photoload technique, we asked the participants to use the photoload sampling protocol to estimate loadings for the six fuel components at the microplot, subplot, and macroplot level. These volunteers had a wide range of fuel sampling experience so we asked them to fill out a questionnaire that documented their personal qualifications and background. These participants consisted of fire managers, scientists, field technicians, and statisticians. A total of 29 participants were randomly assigned to five groups and each group was assigned to one of our five study sites (table 1). Some participants evaluated more than one site. Each participant was given a one hour training session to learn the evaluation methods and to ask questions.

At each of the 25 microplots, each participant used the draft sampling protocol to select the photoload picture that best matched the loading for the 1 hour, 10 hour, 100 hour, shrub, and herbaceous fuels within the portable 1 m² microplot frame placed in the northeast corner of the subplot. To minimize bias, participants were asked not to compare their estimates with those of other participants, but they could ask questions pertaining to procedures and sampling protocols. We also asked them to avoid trampling or disturbing the fuelbed. Unfortunately, the photoload reference book contained only two series of shrub species and two series of grass species so we asked the volunteers to use the photoload series that was most morphologically similar to the shrubs or herbs they were observing in the field.

Participants were then asked to make loading estimates for the 1000 hr woody fuel (logs) at the subplot level (100 m²) (fig. 4). These ocular estimates were made using either the 6 inch or 10 inch log photo sequences. Each participant also had a table (see Keane and Dickinson 2007; RMRS-GTR-190 for the set of tables) that presented loadings for various lengths of logs for both 6 and 10 inch diameter logs. A second table with conversion factors was provided for participants to use so they could accurately adjust the ocular loadings based on the diameters observed in the field (Keane and Dickinson 2007; RMRS-GTR-190).

Participants were then asked to use the photoload reference book to estimate the loading of all six fuel components at the macroplot level (2,500 m²; fig. 4). The participants wandered over the macroplot and selected the picture that best represented the loading across the macroplot as a whole for each fuel component. This was more difficult than the microplot estimates because the fuel components were unevenly distributed across the macroplot and many "jackpots" of fuel were evident. However, this is the scale of sampling that probably will be most often used by fire managers so it was important that we tested and evaluated the photoload technique at this coarser scale. We did not evaluate the photoload technique at the stand level because of logistical difficulties in collecting fuels for the comparison reference data and we felt that the macroplot level was sufficient.

Finally, the participants were asked to write constructive comments on how to improve the reference book design, evaluation sampling method, and plot forms. These comments were compiled into a set of recommendations that were then used to refine the evaluation sampling method into the photoload sampling protocol. We also recorded the time it took for each participant to estimate loadings for all 25 microplots and subplots and the time it took for each participant to estimate loadings at the macroplot level.

Determining actual fuel loadings—The actual fuel loadings were measured after all participants had completed their photoload estimates. It was logistically impractical to collect and weigh all woody fuels for the entire 50x50 meter macroplot because it would have taken a prohibitively long time. And, the log loadings were difficult to accurately measure because they were heavy, unwieldy, and somewhat rotten. We decided to take a sub-sample approach to quantify fuel loadings at the three levels of scale—microplot, subplot, and macroplot.

For the logs, we measured the length, diameter at the small end, and diameter at the large ends of each log that occurred within a subplot. We also estimated the rot class of each log using FIREMON procedures and rot class definitions (Lutes and others 2006). If the log crossed subplot boundaries, length and diameter where the center of the log intersected the subplot edge was measured. Only log and log parts where the center of the log along the longitudinal axis was above the litter layer were measured. The sum of all logs across all 25 subplots provided 100 percent inventory of all logs on the macroplot.

Log loadings were calculated by multiplying log volume by measured wood density. Log volume was calculated using the following formula:

$$V = \frac{l}{3}\left[(a_s + a_l) + \sqrt{(a_s a_l)}\right] \quad (1)$$

where a_s and a_l are the areas of the small and large end of the fuel particle ($a = \pi d^2/4$), respectively (meters) and l is the length of the fuel particle (meters). The wood density was sampled at the site using the same methods described in the Collecting Fuel to Photograph section.

All fine woody material (1 hour, 10 hour, and 100 hour size classes) was removed from each of the 25 microplots. This material was sorted into the three size classes and stored in paper bags for transport to the lab where they were dried and weighed. The live and dead plant material was clipped at ground level, sorted into shrub and herbaceous fuel components, and stored into paper bags that were brought to the lab for drying and weighing. All samples were dried for 3 days in an 80 °C oven and weighed to the nearest milligram. Macroplot loadings were computed as the average loading across all 25 microplots for fine woody material and live fuel components. The data were entered into a database and standard statistical analyses were used to compare the measured loadings with estimates made by field participants using photoload techniques.

Performing the evaluation statistical analysis—To measure the accuracy of the participants in predicting the actual biomass of a particular fuel type at a microplot and macroplot level, we calculated three measures of accuracy: 1) bias, 2) variation between observers, 3) variation within observers. A residual value was calculated for each plot and for each observer. The residual value is calculated as the actual value minus the estimated biomass by the observer. In general, bias is calculated as the average residual; however, because we have a repeated measure design, a mixed effects model was used to estimate the average bias among observers.

The mixed effects model also yields estimates of the variability among observers and also the variability within an observer (in other words, how consistent were the accuracies of particular observers between different plots). We also calculated 95 percent confidence intervals for the mean bias for microplots for the fixed effect parameter (the mean bias among observers) in the mixed effects model. Prediction accuracy was calculated to compare accuracy of fuel components and to evaluate the strength of loading estimations using the photoload technique (Rauscher and others 2000). The prediction accuracy measures the proportion of predictions that fall within a certain percentage of the actual value (Rauscher and others 2000). For example, suppose the actual loading for a fuel component was 0.2 kg m^{-2}. If we were interested in a 10 percent prediction accuracy, we would calculate the proportion of predictions that fell within 10 percent of 0.2 (0.2±0.1*0.2). Percent bias was also computed as the average fuel load for all microplots at a site for a particular fuel component divided by the mean bias at that site.

A nested ANOVA was performed to test for differences between sites and between experience levels (advance, intermediate, and beginner) of the participants using the visually estimated fuel loadings by fuel component as response variables. Observer effect was considered nested within experience level and we considered experience level nested within site. We did this both for the microplot and macroplot estimates. Because of the nested design post hoc tests were not performed for the analysis. Precision and mean square error were also calculated for each fuel component at each site. Precision was calculated as follows:

$$\text{Precision} = \frac{\sum(y_i - \bar{y})^2}{n - 1} \quad (2)$$

where y_i is the estimated biomass for participant i and $\bar{y}$ is equal to the mean of all estimates at that particular microplot. The mean square error (MSE) is used to measure the performance of a model's prediction and is calculated by summing the bias squared and the variance.

Developing the Photoload Sampling Protocol

The testing and evaluation process revealed a number of limitations and flaws in the photoload sampling technique that needed to be addressed before developing a final sampling protocol. We used the comments provided by the participants, along with our own observations, to refine the evaluation procedures to create a sampling protocol for others to use for sampling loading.

The photoload sampling protocol includes many tips, options, and short-cuts that may help, improve, and refine photoload loading estimates. We used the structure and format of FIREMON to organize and write the sampling protocol. Our hope was that people could read this protocol and teach themselves how to estimate loadings with only an hour of field training.

Results

Photoload Sequences and Sampling Protocol

The final set of photoload sequences that were developed for all six fuel components are shown in the companion document RMRS-GTR-190 (Keane and Dickinson 2007) and an example of a photoload sequence is shown in figure 5 for the 1 hr down woody fuel component. The photoload sequences for all fuel components are present

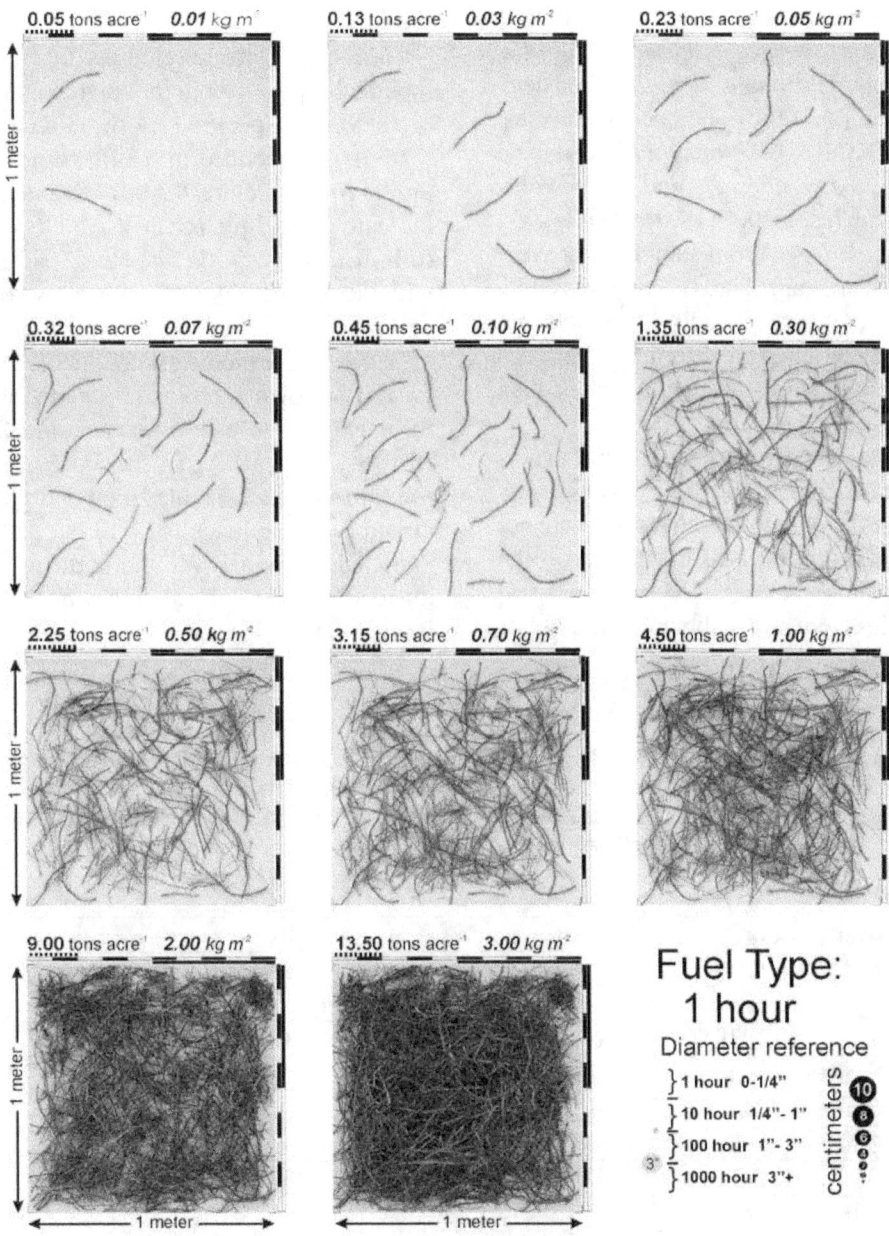

Figure 5—An example of a photoload sequence for the 1 hr fuel component.

in digital files on this CD in the directory /photoloads for reference. The original photoload reference books used over 20 photographs to portray the range of fuel loadings for any component. The evaluators found that it was often difficult to distinguish differences in fine fuel loadings between pictures, so some intermediate photos were removed to create a smaller set of nine for most fuel components. This seemed to better match the resolution detectable with the human eye. The loading for the fuel in each picture is provided in both English and metric units but the fuelbeds were built to hold even intervals of the metric measurement (intervals of kg m^{-2}).

For the live fuels, there are seven sets of photoload sequences for shrub species (*Amelanchier alnifolia, Berberis repens, Physocarpus malvaceus, Spiraea betulifolia, Symphorocarpus albus, Vaccinium globulare,* and *Vaccinium scoparium*) and four sets for herbaceous species: two forbs (*Arnica latifolia* and *Xerophyllum tenax*) and two grasses (*Calamagrostis rubescens* and *Festuca scabrella*) (Keane and Dickinson 2007; RMRS-GTR-190). These sequences were created from samples that were collected in the forests and rangelands around Missoula, Montana. Again, the sequence of loadings was selected primarily based on the recognizable differences between fuelbeds across the entire series of pictures rather than discrete loading classes.

The densities of the wood found on all five evaluation sites are presented in table 2. Density of woody fuels photographed in the photoload sequences were not significantly different from the densities found on the accuracy assessment sites (p<0.05). However, the 1 and 10 hour wood densities were noticeably high because of inaccuracies in the measurement of the small and highly variable twig diameters (table 2), so we used the 100 hour wood densities for these fine wood components in our analysis.

The photoload sampling protocol developed from this study is detailed in the companion document Keane and Dickinson (2007; RMRS-GTR-190). This protocol is an extensive refinement of the procedures used in the photoload evaluation effort. It has been further tested and refined using the comments and suggestions from the evaluation participants. The protocol document was designed so that the photoload sequences can be removed from the report, laminated, and then taken into the field.

The entire suite of pictures taken for this study is included on this CD in the /pictures directory. The type of fuelbed is specified by the directory name and the loading is embedded in the filename. For example, the digital file in /pictures/forbs/arnica/above/0.08kg would indicate that the picture is of a fuelbed composed of the forb *Arnica cordifolia* that has a loading of 0.08 kg m^{-2} with the pictures taken directly above or overhead (most herb and shrub fuelbeds also have pictures taken from the side). These pictures were put on the CD so users can create their own photoload reference sheet in a different format than that used in Keane and Dickinson (2007; RMRS-GTR-190). Again, the entire set of final photoloads (picture sequences) is also included as digital files in the directory /photoloads for reference and printing. Also included on the CD are the tables used for estimating log loading from log length (Keane and Dickinson 2007; RMRS-GTR-190).

Table 2—Average wood density (kg m^{-3}) by woody size and rot class for each of the five sites included in this study. Dashes indicate that the fuel type was not encountered on that site. The term "all" is used to identify that all rot classes were used to calculate the mean density. Rot class categories are defined in Lutes and others (2006).

Woody fuel component	Wood rot class	Site				
		1	2	3	4	5
		Wood density (kg m^{-3})				
1 hr	All	676	885	918	722	--
10 hr	All	496	539	544	549	435
100 hr	All	435	382	406	406	497
1000 hr	1	--	--	--	--	--
1000 hr	2	392	433	459	359	431
1000 hr	3	348	541	371	338	356
1000 hr	4	404	356	--	--	311
1000 hr	5	--	287	--	--	--

Photoload Evaluation

Microplot level—Overall, the evaluators usually underestimated fine fuel loadings on the 1 m² microplot using the photoload technique with an average bias of 0.182 kg m⁻² (0.8 tons acre⁻¹) (table 3). Underestimates result in positive biases even though this seems counterintuitive. Although photoload estimates consistently underestimated actual fuel loadings, we found that the error of the estimate seemed to be within the resolution required by the computer models for which these estimates are used for inputs (Lutes 1999; Lutes [in prep]). The accuracy of the photoload estimates depended on fuel component with bias ranging from 0.0002 kg m⁻²

(0.0009 tons acre⁻¹) for herbaceous fuels and 2.69 kg m⁻² (11.96 tons acre⁻¹) for logs (summarized from table 3). The average of residuals and variance are near zero for most of the fuel components except for the larger woody material (10, 100, and 1000 hour fuels). However, the variations of the estimates across evaluators and sites were high (fig. 6). In general, there was much more variation between plots than there was variation between observers (table 3).

As mentioned, most evaluators tended to underestimate actual fuel loadings using the photoload protocols, especially for larger woody fuels (fig. 6), and this underestimation usually increased with increasing fuel loadings

Table 3—The accuracy of photoload estimates averaged across all field participants for each site over all the microplots (subplots for log material). The variable n refers to the number of estimates from all participants across all microplots for the site. We removed those microplots where the measured loadings were zero. PA-10 and PA-50 are the precision accuracies at the 10 and 50 percent level, which indicate the proportion of observations (n) that fell within 10 and 50 percent of the mean loading.

Site	Component	N	n	Bias (kg m⁻²)	95% confidence interval for bias (kg m⁻²)	Variation between observers (kg m⁻²)	Variation within observers (kg m⁻²)	Bias (%)	PA-10	PA-50
1	1 hour	5	44	-.0015	(-.0042,.0012)	.0023	.0056	29.24	0.09	0.27
	10 hour	5	88	.142	(.106,.177)	8.8 x 10⁻⁷	.167	85.90	0.02	0.09
	100 hour	4	16	.103	(.019,.187)	.000091	.154	33.61	0.25	0.50
	Logs	5	82	.142	(.090,.194)	.000001	.236	25.63	0.11	0.40
	Herbs	5	84	.014	(.0011,.0274)	.000031	.060	54.44	0.13	0.45
	Shrubs	4	4	.0002					0.00	0.00
2	1 hour	9	103	-.005	(-.009,-.0004)	.006	.009	186.89	0.03	0.15
	10 hour	9	216	.101	(.088,.114)	.000012	.099	77.89	0.01	0.14
	100 hour	9	69	.106	(.066,.146)	.027	.150	52.56	0.04	0.45
	Logs	9	196	.100	(.034,.166)	.088	.223	16.68	0.09	0.69
	Herbs	9	208	.012	(-.0014,.0248)	.015	.062	25.60	0.13	0.55
	Shrubs	9	9	-.003	(-.008,.003)	.0065	.0024	71.43	0.00	0.44
3	1 hour	14	328	.055	(.038,.073)	.000012	.164	46.07	0.09	0.41
	10 hour	14	341	.300	(.261,.340)	.000013	.367	68.43	0.02	0.12
	100 hour	14	218	.359	(.213,.505)	.208	.720	40.50	0.05	0.27
	Logs	14	288	.092	(.033,.150)	.083	.334	0.86	0.12	0.61
	Herbs	14	313	.0004	(-.014,.144)	.014	.106	20.60	0.17	0.58
	Shrubs	14	218	.009	(.005,.013)	.000028	.030	45.66	0.04	0.25
4	1 hour	11	170	-.005	(-.013,.003)	.009	.036	31.45	0.04	0.16
	10 hour	11	169	.063	(.047,.079)	.004	.104	57.10	0.04	0.22
	100 hour	11	65	.142	(.006,.279)	.117	.471	30.90	0.09	0.37
	Logs	11	252	-.152	(-.257,-.047)	.126	.594	54.83	0.13	0.53
	Herbs	10	209	-.036	(-.050,-.023)	.00008	.098	25.49	0.10	0.52
	Shrubs	11	224	.035	(.015,.056)	.012	.145	45.29	0.05	0.21
5	1 hour	8	186	-.003	(-.062,.056)	.030	.381	1.04	0.04	0.33
	10 hour	8	194	.242	(.148..337)	.075	.554	43.72	0.03	0.19
	100 hour	8	145	.553	(.349,.757)	.232	.753	54.42	0.06	0.26
	Logs	8	177	2.69	(1.84,3.55)	.0002	5.748	40.40	0.03	0.29
	Herbs	8	170	.029	(.010,.048)	.000008	.124	71.16	0.02	0.24
	Shrubs	8	147	-.0015	(-.012,.0084)	.00003	.061	13.99	0.06	0.22

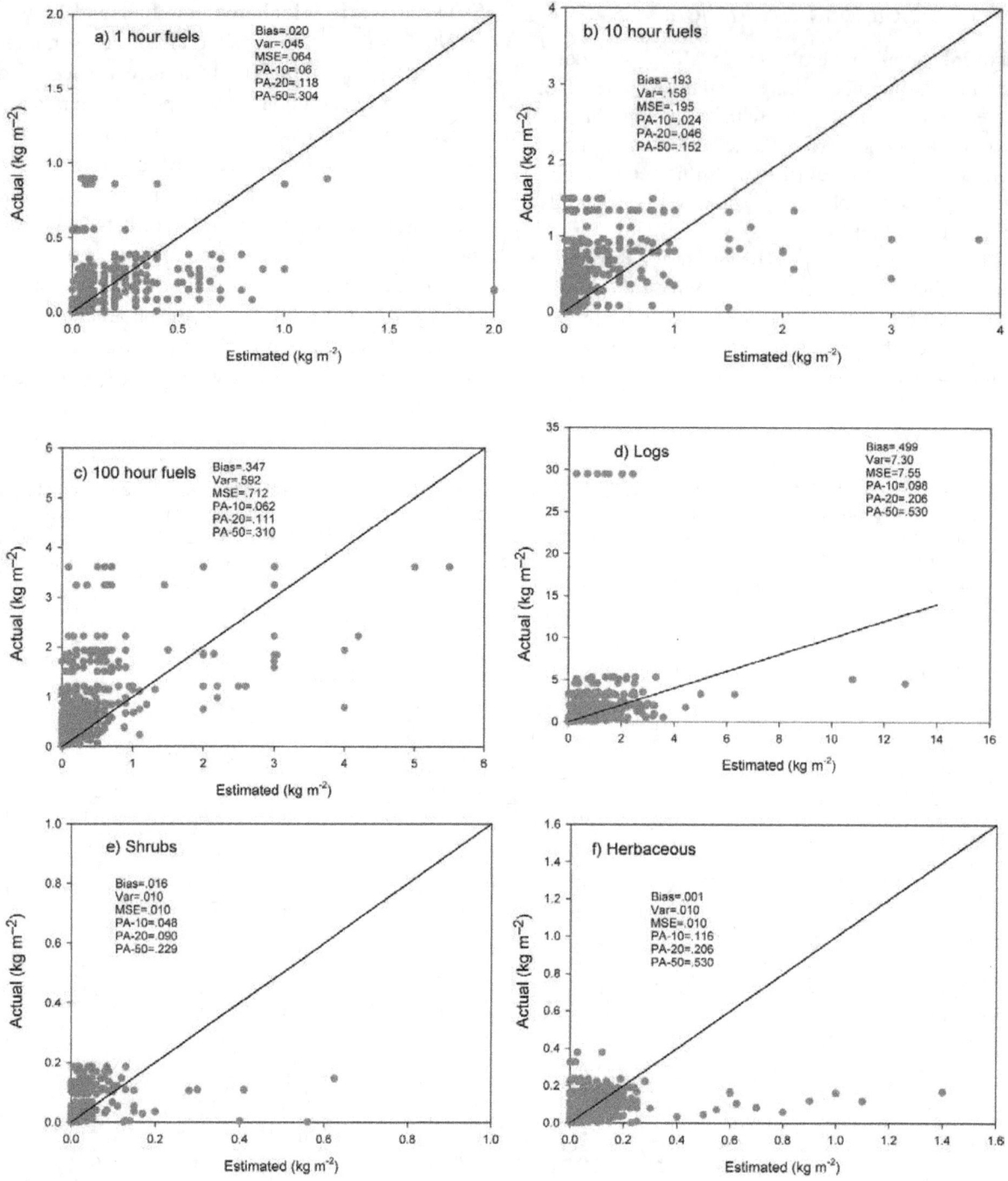

Figure 6—Scatterplots showing actual loadings versus estimated loadings at the microplot level using the photoload method for all six fuel components: a) 1 hour dead woody, b) 10 hour dead woody, c) 100 hour dead woody, d) logs or 1000 hour dead woody, e) live and dead shrub, and f) live and dead herbaceous.

(see scatter of residuals in fig. 7). Based on confidence intervals (table 3), it appears that observed values for 1 hour herbs and shrubs may be unbiased and therefore somewhat accurate. The confidence intervals included zero for three out of five of the sites for 1 hour woody fuels and two out of five for herbaceous fuels. For shrubs, the intervals contained zero for two out of five sites. Confidence intervals for the 10 hour fuels were positive for all sites and none of the intervals contained zero. In general, the lightest fuel loads were overestimated with photoload techniques while the heavier fuel loads were underestimated.

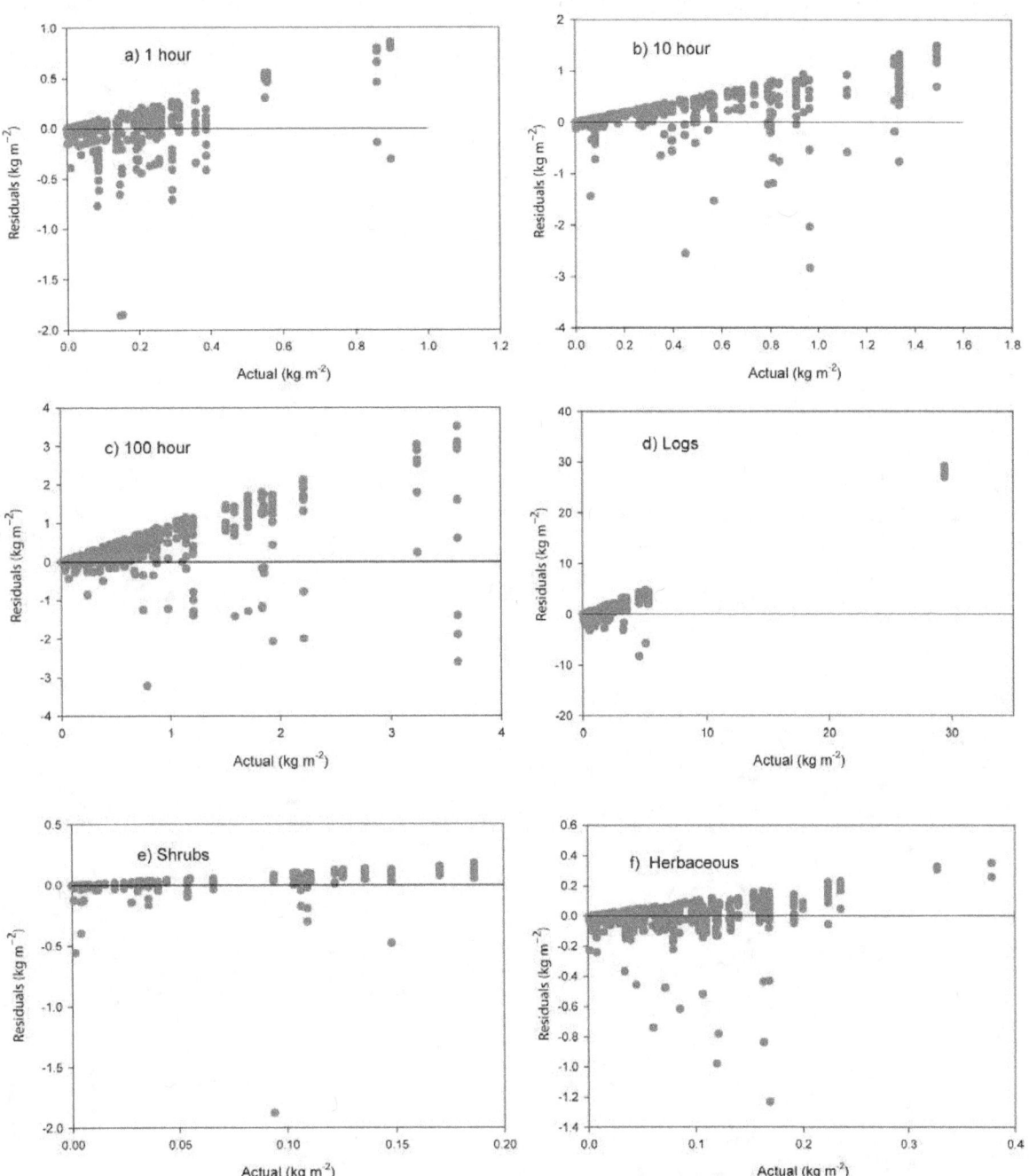

Figure 7—Scatterplots of residual versus actual values at the microplot level for the six fuel components when the loadings estimated by the photoload technique were compared to actual loadings at the microplot scale. Fuel components are a) 1 hour dead woody, b) 10 hour dead woody, c) 100 hour dead woody, d) logs or 1000 hour dead woody, e) live and dead shrub, and f) live and dead herbaceous.

The high variability in evaluator estimates at the microplot level contributed to a low precision where only 6 of 30 site-fuel component comparisons had 50 percent of the observations occurring within 50 percent of the actual measured value (see the column PA-50 in table 3). Only one site-component combination (Cayuse 1 for 100 hour woody) had over 25 percent of the estimates within 10 percent of the actual value. The highest fuel loadings (Site 5-logs) also had the poorest performance for photoload methods because it had the highest bias and variance within observer (table 3).

Within a site, the experience level did not have a significant effect on accuracy at any of the sites. However, the distribution of the residuals stratified by experience level (fig. 8) shows that, although the means were not significantly different, the variance tends to decrease with

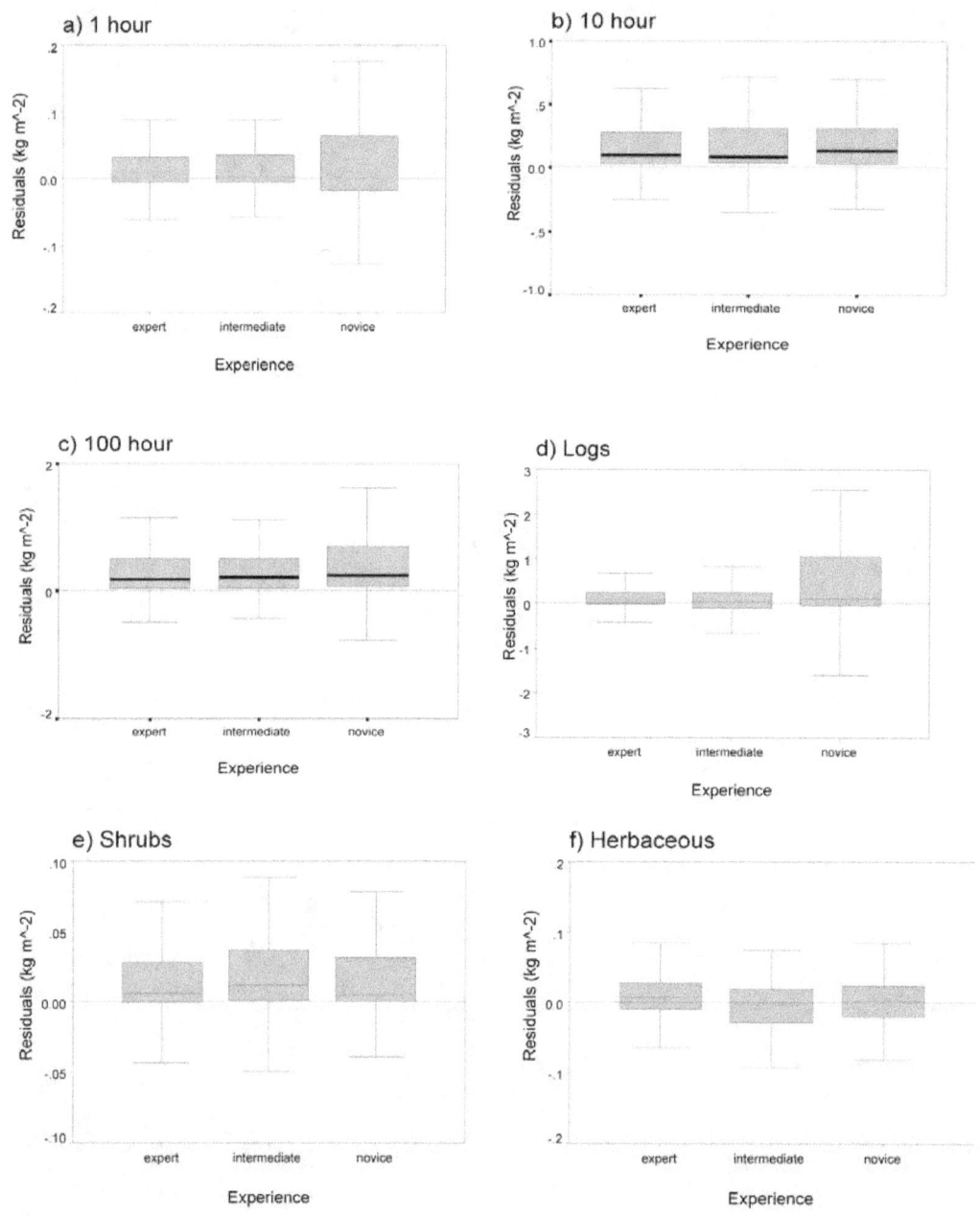

Figure 8—Boxplots of residuals (actual-estimated) computed at the microplot level stratified by the three levels of fuel sampling experience of the evaluation participants by each of the six fuel components: a) 1 hour dead woody, b) 10 hour dead woody, c) 100 hour dead woody, d) logs or 1000 hour dead woody, e) live and dead shrub, and f) live and dead herbaceous.

increasing fuel sampling experience, especially for 1, 100, and 1000 hour fuels. People with high expertise in fuel sampling experts tend to have more precise estimations. Herbaceous and shrub fuels are the components where this may not be true, probably because the photoload evaluation book did not always have pictures of the same species that occurred on the microplots.

Site was a significant factor influencing the accuracy of the photoload estimates for all of the six fuel components (table 4; p-value < 0.05) at the microplots. This is primarily because the fuelbed is different in loading and composition between sites (table 1) and the bias and variance of the photoload estimates tended to increase with increasing loadings (table 1 and fig. 7). The differences in bias by site are shown in figure 9 where the high fuel loadings on Site 5 (Moncure) are associated with greater means of the residuals causing significant differences in estimates. The variability of the residuals for the six fuel components is also different across sites because of the high diversity in fuel loadings across sites (table 1). It appears that the significant differences between sites are

probably due to the influence of one site that had high fuel loadings (Moncure, site 5). Site differences in fine woody fuels are primarily a result of the difference between activity and natural fuelbeds for the sites (activity fuelbeds have substantially more woody debris).

Evaluators averaged approximately 6.3 minutes per microplot to estimate loadings of all fuel components including the time it took to estimate log loadings at the subplot level. Times for microplot estimates ranged from 2.7 minutes for the most experienced evaluators to over 10.1 minutes for novice fuel samplers. These times tended to increase with increasing loadings with the longest times for the slash sites (Moncure 5 average was 7.2 minutes) and heavy fuel units (6.3 minutes for Kries 4). Sites with light fuel loadings had the shortest evaluation times (4.2 minutes for Cayuse 1). Times for most people decreased as more microplots were evaluated, especially for the subplot estimates of log loadings, as people learned how to efficiently use the log loading table. One participant's sampling time decreased by more than 70 percent after 50 microplots.

Table 4—Results of the ANOVA at the microplot (subplot for logs) and macroplot level showing the significance of site and experience. Numbers in bold indicate significance (p<0.05). Sampling site was significant for four fuel components at the microplot scale compared to one fuel component at the macroplot scale. Level of experience was important only for herbaceous fuels at both scales of estimation in accurately estimating loading using the photoload method.

Component	Variable	Df	Microplot		Df	Macroplot	
			F-value	p-value		F-value	p-value
1 hour	Site	4	2.873	**.032**	4	.358	.837
	Experience (Site)	8	.161	.995	9	3.161	**.008**
	Observer (Experience (Site))	34	.989	.488			
10 hour	Site	4	15.534	**<.001**	4	2.241	.087
	Experience (Site)	8	.280	.969	9	2.594	**.023**
	Observer (Experience (Site))	34	1.067	.366			
100 hour	Site	4	4.265	**.006**	4	1.321	.283
	Experience (Site)	8	.241	.980	9	2.365	**.035**
	Observer (Experience (Site))	33	2.012	**.001**			
1000 hour (logs)	Site	4	76.821	**<.001**	4	39.337	**<.001**
	Experience (Site)	8	.170	.996	9	2.226	**.047**
	Observer (Experience (Site))	32	.437	.997			
Herbs	Site	4	10.183	**<.001**	4	2.142	.098
	Experience (Site)	8	1.201	.326	9	1.555	.171
	Observer (Experience (Site))	33	1.208	.197			
Shrubs	Site	4	5.241	**.001**	4	.071	.931
	Experience (Site)	8	.452	.883	9	1.353	.275
	Observer (Experience (Site))	32	.714	.879			

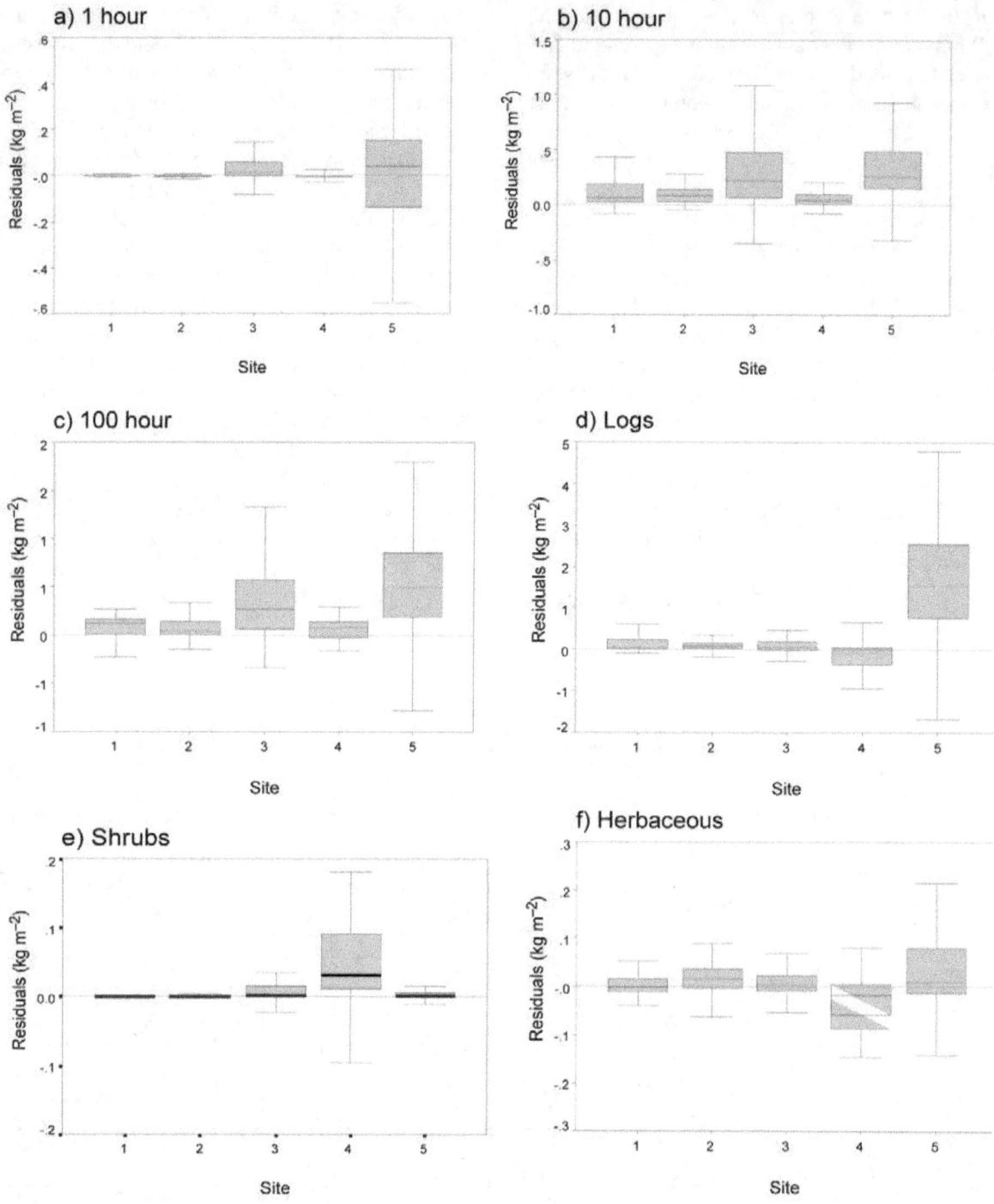

Figure 9—Boxplots of residuals (actual-estimated) computed at the microplot level stratified by the five sites for each of the six fuel components: a) 1 hour dead woody, b) 10 hour dead woody, c) 100 hour dead woody, d) logs or 1000 hour dead woody, e) live and dead shrub, and f) live and dead herbaceous

USDA Forest Service Res. Pap. RMRS-RP-61CD. 2007

Macroplot level—The scatter of residuals of photoload evaluator estimates at the macroplot level is quite similar to the microplot evaluation results for most fuel components (compare fig. 10 with fig. 6). However, the estimates of fuel loading obtained by surveying the entire macroplot are less accurate (error is 0.0418 vs. 0.0177 kg m^{-2} for microplot) but more precise (bias is 0.0476 vs. 0.182 kg m^{-2} for microplot) than the microplot estimates. The bias for nearly every fuel component was less for macroplot estimates, except for shrub (–0.0045 kg m^{-2}) and herbaceous (–0.0043 kg m^{-2}) (this is probably because of an evaluator mistake in recording loading for shrubs and herbs). Negative bias for shrub, herb, 1 hour woody (–0.0093 kg m^{-2}), and 100 hour woody (–0.144 kg m^{-2})

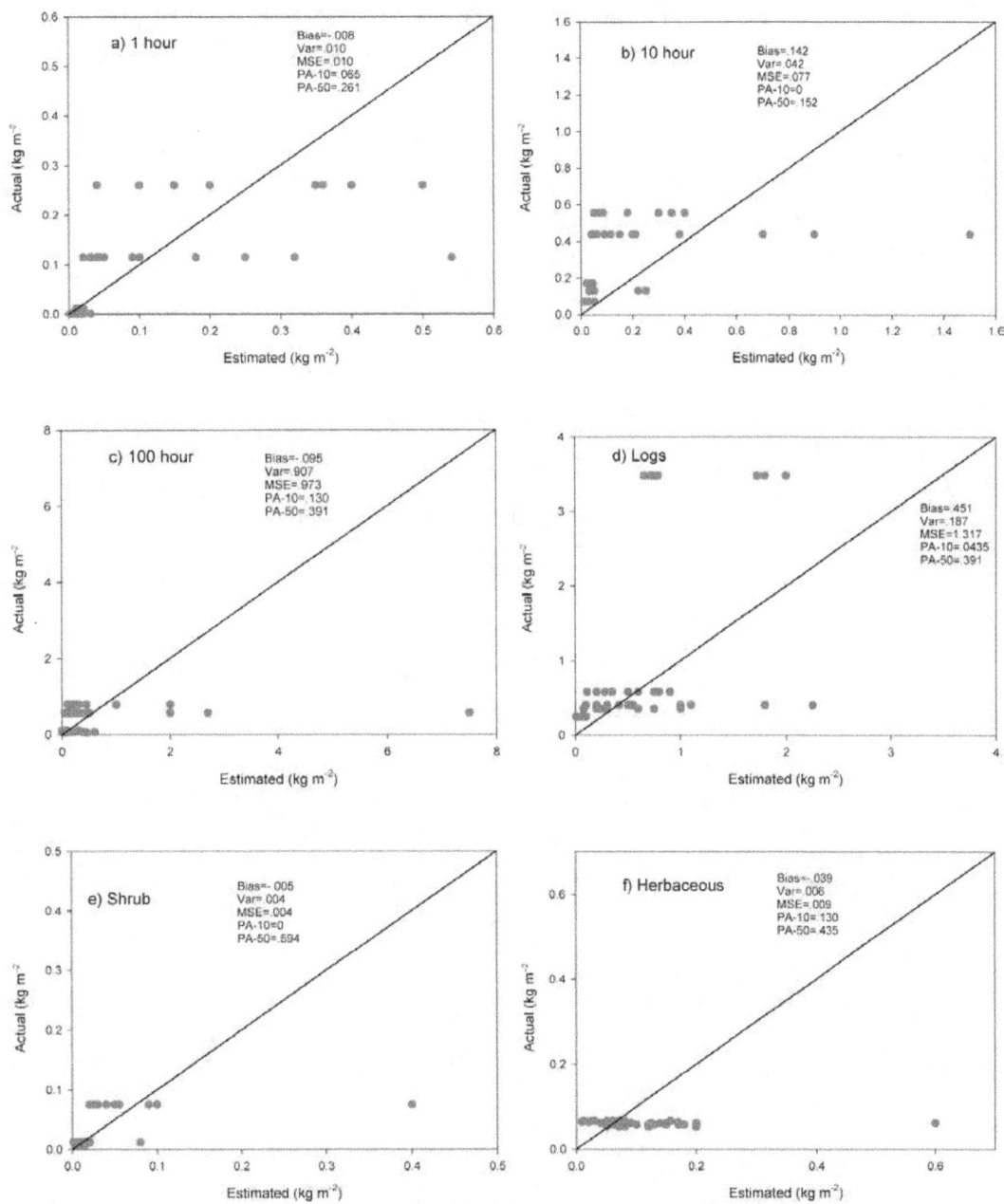

Figure 10—Scatterplots showing actual loadings versus estimated loadings at the *macroplot level* using the photoload method for all six fuel components: a) 1 hour dead woody, b) 10 hour dead woody, c) 100 hour dead woody, d) logs or 1000 hour dead woody, e) live and dead shrub, and f) live and dead herbaceous.

indicates that evaluators overestimated macroplot-level loadings. Curiously, the 100 hour woody fuel estimates had the greatest error (0.169 kg m^{-2}) with logs coming in a close second (0.155 kg m^{-2}). The next highest error for 10 hour (0.039 kg m^{-2}) was nearly a fourth lower than the larger fuels. This was presumably because of the highly clustered nature of 100 hour fuels and logs on our sites. Macroplot log loadings had similar bias when compared to the subplot estimates (0.339 kg m^{-2} for subplot and 0.499 kg m^{-2} for macroplot) but macroplot errors were nearly double (0.155 vs. 0.084 kg m^{-2}).

As in the microplot evaluations, the novice evaluators had less precise (higher variability) macroplot loading estimates for nearly all fuel components except for shrub and herbs (fig. 11). There were also significant differences between expertise levels within a site for four of the six fuel components (table 4). It appears that the novice is able to estimate loadings with the same level of accuracy and precision as the expert across a large area. The significant differences between experience level within a site is probably because many of our participants had never attempted to rate fuel loadings across such a large

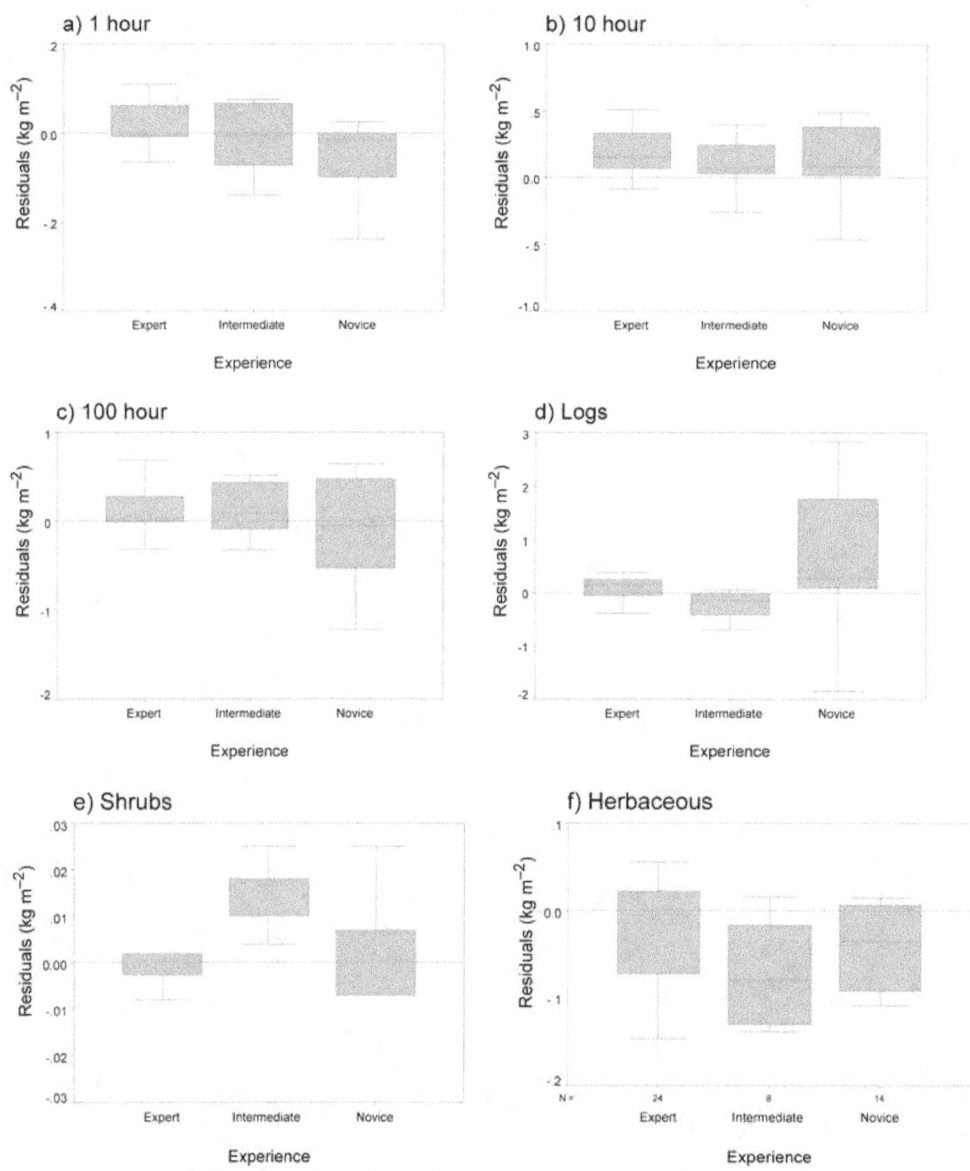

Figure 11—Boxplots of residuals (actual-estimated) at the macroplot level stratified by the level of expertise of the evaluation participants for each of the six fuel components: a) 1 hour dead woody, b) 10 hour dead woody, c) 100 hour dead woody, d) logs or 1000 hour dead woody, e) live and dead shrub, and f) live and dead herbaceous.

USDA Forest Service Res. Pap. RMRS-RP-61CD. 2007

area with photos of small, one square meter plots. It was difficult for them to account for spatial distribution of fuels (clumping, jackpots) in the final estimate. It was also interesting that the wide range of estimates shown in figure 10 is independent of fuel sampling expertise.

The significant differences in accuracy between sites for 10 hr, 100 hr, shrubs and herbaceous fuels observed for the microplot evaluation were not evident in the macroplot comparison (table 4), although the accuracy of the loading estimates was related to site for logs and 10 hour fuels. This is probably because of large woody fuels have the lowest differences in loadings among the sites (table 1). It appears that the four woody fuel components (1, 10, 100, 1000 hour) have less variation in the residuals for all but site 3 (Sawmill) and site 5 (Moncure) (fig. 12). The fuelbeds for both sites had activity fuels of high fuel loadings, especially in the fine woody components. Estimates for the Moncure site are the least accurate of all sites, probably due to the high fuel loadings. Evaluators took 5.1 to over 10 minutes to estimate loadings of all six surface fuel components for the entire macroplot.

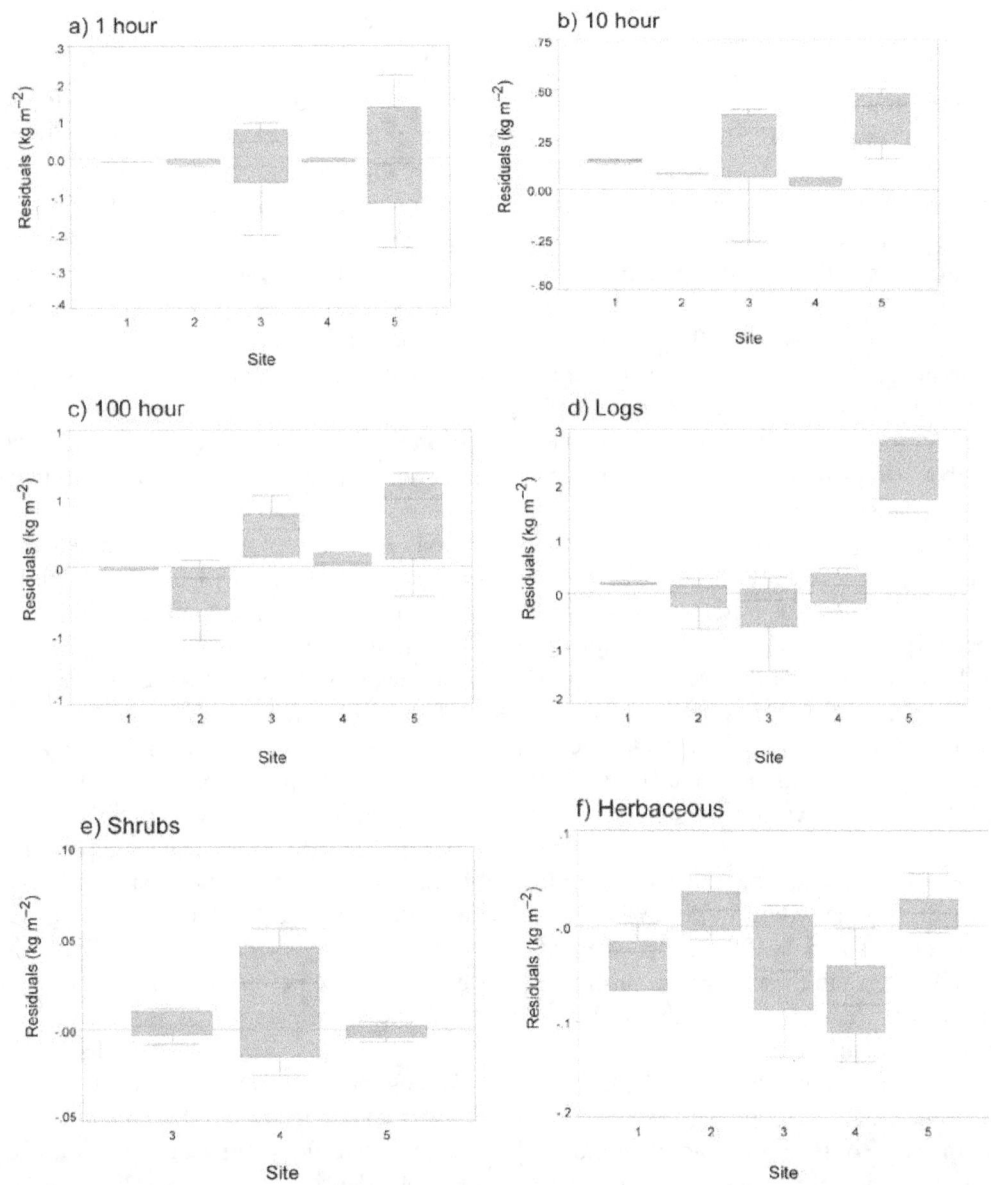

Figure 12—Boxplots of residuals (actual-estimated) at the macroplot level stratified by the five sites in the study for each of the six fuel components: a) 1 hour dead woody, b) 10 hour dead woody, c) 100 hour dead woody, d) logs or 1000 hour dead woody, e) live and dead shrub, and f) live and dead herbaceous.

Discussion

Evaluation of the Photoload Technique

In general, visual estimates made using the photoload technique were reasonably accurate for most fuel components, especially when the experience of the sampler was high. Accuracy was highest when the fuel loadings were the lightest, probably because relative differences in observed and estimated values tended to be smaller when loadings were low. Most participants tended to underestimate loadings for nearly all fuel components except the fine fuels of 1 hour and herbaceous vegetation, and these underestimations got larger as the fuel loadings increased (positive values in fig. 7). Moreover, the variability of the estimations increased with fuel loading. This could have definitely been improved by a more intensive and improved training session. We believe the estimations would have been more accurate if we had previously measured actual fuel loadings on some demonstration microplots and used these demonstration microplots to calibrate the evaluator's estimations. We also believe that the training should have involved an expert accompanying the novice to evaluate at least 10-15 microplots to ensure that the novice's estimates have included all appropriate adjustments (see Keane and Dickinson 2007; RMRS-GTR-190 for details). Accuracy and precision could have also been improved if there were multiple evaluators at a site to check each other's work.

Average bias of the estimated fuel loadings (actual-estimated) was not statistically significant across evaluator fuel sampling experience, but the variance differed by experience, especially at the microplot level (residuals in figs. 8 and 11). This suggests that the precision of photoload estimates increases as one gets more experience in fuel sampling but the accuracy might not improve; as people become more familiar with photoload estimation and gain valuable field experience, the resultant estimates will probably be more repeatable (greater precision) but there seems to be a limit on accuracy in our group of evaluators. However, accuracy could improve with experience for an individual especially if there are sufficient calibration microplots to train the eye. Future testing is needed to assess the accuracy of a person that had been using the photoload technique for years.

Estimates made across a larger extent (macroplot) had better precision but less accuracy (greater bias) than estimates made at the scale of the photoload photographs (microplot). This is probably the result of a combination of factors. First, none of the evaluators, even the most experienced fuel samplers, had experience in using small scale photos for assessing large scale loadings. Second, there were significantly more observations (25 times) for evaluator microplot estimates than macroplot estimates because each site only had one macroplot evaluator estimate. This large difference in observations might tend to skew results. Third, the evaluators performed macroplot estimates after they had completed the 25 microplot estimates for a site. The additional training and the prior knowledge of macroplot conditions from microplot sampling might have contributed to high precision in macroplot estimates. Last, the measurement of actual loadings did not match the scale of macroplot estimates (see next section). We believe that the microplot represents the best sampling frame for the most accurate and repeatable photoload estimates (except for logs) even though bias for microplots was higher.

Limitations of the photoload evaluation—We found that the majority of estimation error from the evaluation participants was a result of inaccurate recording of the estimates on the plot form rather than actual errors of estimation using the technique. People wrote the wrong number on the plot sheet for a number of reasons. Confusion with the decimal point (for example, 0.1 loading was written when they really meant to write 0.01) was a major cause of recording error, but we also found that people were recording shrub loadings in herbaceous loading plot form fields, or they were recording the wrong microplot or subplot number on the plot form, mostly because of confusion in understanding our plot layout (fig. 4). We tried to catch most of these errors while the participants were on site but many mistakes went undetected. Therefore, it is important that photoload users pay attention to the smallest details when recording estimates in the field and make sure each of their entries are correct.

It was difficult to train all evaluation participants to the same level of expertise in using the photoload technique because of the great disparity in fuel sampling experience among participants. Some participants had never sampled fuels in the field so they needed extra training to familiarize them with the identification of woody size classes and fuel components. Others had extensive fuel sampling experience so they needed much less training and had a greater proficiency in photoload sampling. This is why the variance was greater when estimates are made by novice evaluators (figs. 8 and 11). The disparity in the level of training may have influenced these evaluation results.

The actual measured fuel loadings that were used as reference for comparing the evaluator's macroplot photoload estimates had some limitations that may have influenced the comparison results. The only fuel component that was measured on the entire macroplot (100% sample) was logs (1000 hour downed dead woody). We used a sub-sample approach to quantify the remaining fuel component loadings where only one percent of the total macroplot area was sampled. This was because it was too costly and difficult to clip, collect, dry, and weigh all fuels across the entire macroplot on all sites. As a result, the reference estimates of fine fuel components may not have adequately described plot-wide fuel loadings.

The measured density of the woody material also influenced the reference fuel loadings in a number of ways. First, measured densities for the fine woody components were high because of difficulty estimating volume for the small, non-uniform twigs. The diameters of the small twigs were highly variable along their length and the twigs were sometimes crooked and irregular. We should have used the liquid displacement method (van Wagtendonk and others 1996) but we had no time to build this apparatus. The densities were highly variable both within and across fuel types making it difficult to select an appropriate density to use for calculating loadings, especially the small woody material. We had to use densities calculated for the 100 hour branches for the 1 and 10 hour twigs.

Most of the microplots on four of the sites had very light fuel loadings resulting in the majority of the comparisons having fuels that were less than 0.1 kg m^{-2}. Over 80 percent of the microplots had light fuel loading estimates (<0.10 kg m^{-2}), so the distribution of loading estimates is somewhat skewed towards low loading values and doesn't fully capture the range contained in the photoload sequences. As a result, the photoload technique may not have been adequately tested across the full range of fuel loadings found in the field. It is important that users of photoload perform their own evaluations on fuelbeds that they create to ensure the highest accuracy in ocular estimation. The photoload sequences presented in Keane and Dickinson (2007; RMRS-GTR-190) may not adequately represent the full range of loadings in slash fuels so the user might need to take photos of additional fuelbeds.

The shrub and herbaceous species encountered on some of the sample sites did not match the species in the photoload evaluation book; the evaluator had to pick the best match and this was often difficult for a number of reasons. First, the photoload reference book only had grass species in the photoload sequences with no forb species. Many forbs occurred on the plots and the evaluators used the grass pictures to estimate forb loadings with limited success. We have since included forb species in the photoload sequences. For shrubs, several species growing on the plots were not present in the book so we had to select the best match. Morphological

differences between pictured and on-site species probably contributed to high evaluator error. For example, spiraea (*Spiraea betulifolia*) loadings were much lower than ninebark (*Physocarpus malvaceus*) loadings even though their height and cover were roughly the same.

Another problem in using the photoload sampling technique for shrub and herbaceous fuels is that the phenological changes that plants experience during the year may make it difficult to consistently estimate loadings. Green grasses, for example, appear quite different when they are cured, and shrub loadings depend on whether the leaves are on or shed. To compensate for phenological changes, we suggest that photoload users try to match the phenological stage of the evaluation to the application of the collected fuels data. If the collected data are to be used to determine fire behavior and effects for a fall burn, for example, then the field sampler should try to visually adjust loadings to match for autumnal phenological conditions. This means the user must attempt to increase or decrease ocular assessments to match the desired phenological stage.

These detailed limitations suggest the following recommendations and future improvements for the photoload technique:

- Implement an extensive quality control/quality assessment procedure to minimize user-controlled data collection errors.
- Extensively train field personnel to ensure consistency of estimates. This training should include the following for users to calibrate their visual estimates:
  o A tutorial could be developed that shows various natural fuelbeds with various loadings.
  o Fuelbeds of known loadings should be created in the field to train photoload users.
  o The first efforts at estimating fuels should include double sampling where every tenth estimate should be destructively sampled to measure actual fuel loadings. Regression techniques can be used to develop an adjustment factor and to evaluate the quality of estimates. Photos of sampled fuelbeds can be used for training.
- Comprehensively describe the distribution of wood densities across various species, decay classes, and particle sizes so that estimates can be adjusted to more accurately determine fuel loadings.
- Describe the spatial distribution of the fuel components to more accurately and comprehensively determine the appropriate scale of sampling for each fuel component.

- Create additional photoload sequences for shrub and herbaceous species not photographed in this study, especially for rangelands and woodlands, and include adjustments for phenological stages.
- Create photoload sequences for larger log diameters and include adjustments for decay.
- Create photoload sequences for slash fuels and blowdown.

Using the Photoload Sampling Technique in the Field

There are many subtleties and pitfalls in estimating fuel loadings using visual estimates that preclude someone from simply taking the photoload sequences provided in Keane and Dickinson (2007; RMRS-GTR-190) and going directly into the field to estimate loadings. Adjustments to ocular estimates must be made for many sampling factors such as fuel spatial distribution, rot, depth, and sampling scale. We developed a comprehensive set of procedures to use with the photoload sequences so that the ocular estimates of fuel loadings have higher accuracy and precision (photoload sampling protocol as described in Keane and Dickinson 2007; RMRS-GTR-190).

The photoload sampling protocol was designed to be used at multiple sampling scales (microplot to macroplot to stand to landscape levels) and at various levels of effort (quick to time-consuming). Use of photoload techniques at the microplot scale would involve nearly the same procedures that were presented for the evaluation effort. However, use of the photoload technique at other spatial scales involves either the installation of a systematic network of microplots to estimate loadings or a reconnaissance of the area to make one estimate of loading for the entire area (the macroplot evaluation method described in previous sections). Obviously, more microplots would be needed as the sampling area increases, as the fuels became more heterogeneous and as higher accuracies are desired, and at some point there might be a need to stratify the microplot network by other biophysical characteristics. We found that, although smaller sampling frames result in more accurate photoload estimates, the loss in accuracy as sampling frame size increases is not that great for areas less than the macroplot size used in this study (0.25 ha or 0.62 acres). Listed next are some recommendations and limitations.

Recommendations for using the photoload technique—The ability of the sampler to consistently estimate woody fuels is mostly dependent on their level of expertise (figs. 8 and 11). Therefore, users of the photoload technique must calibrate their eye so that they can consistently and accurately estimate loadings. Ocular calibration to improve accuracy and precision of loading estimates can be done by repeating our methods for measuring the reference fuel loading conditions in the evaluation of the photoload technique (see Methods section). We suggest the use of 1x1 meter square plot frames in the field to estimate loadings using the photoload sampling protocol, followed by the collection and measurement of fuel components. Comparisons of measured loadings with ocular estimates will identify potential estimator bias and inaccuracies. We also suggest that the users take photos of the 1x1 meter frames so that they can compare their measured loadings with the photoload pictures to calibrate their eye for future field seasons or to teach the photoload technique to others.

Another way to calibrate photoload woody fuel estimates is to define a plot of known area and install a number of transects to measure woody fuel using the planar intersect (see Lutes and others 2006; FIREMON). We suggest that at least 5-10 transects be established within the defined area and 5-10 microplots (1x1 meter plot frame) be installed on each transect to get the most accurate woody fuel loadings. Refer to FIREMON for the most appropriate field sampling procedures (Lutes and others 2006). The computed woody fuel loadings by size class can be compared to photoload estimates for the defined area. Again, pictures should be taken of the plot and fuel conditions to document the fuelbed conditions for future training use.

The depth of the fuelbed must be accounted for in all photoload estimates and especially shrub and herb components. Fortunately, woody fuels on most fuelbeds have shallow depths under natural conditions. However, shrub and herb fuelbeds have depth (measured as average vegetation height in this study) and this dimension must be included in the photoload process to adjust for the ocular estimate. Each of the pictures for shrub and herb fuelbeds in the photoload sequences documents a height of the plant material, which is the height that we measured when we constructed the fuelbeds to be photographed. We suggest that once the photoload picture is matched to the fuel conditions in the field and the loading has been determined, then that estimate should be adjusted by multiplying the amount by the proportional change in height from the picture to the observed fuelbed. For example, if the photoload shrub height is 1 meter and the matched loading is 2.0 kg m^{-2} but the observed height of the shrubs in the field is 2 meters, then the actual loading would be 4.0 kg m^{-2} (2.0 kg m^{-2} x 2 meters / 1 meter). If the litter surface is not visible for estimating high downed dead woody loadings, as is the case in slash and activity fuelbeds, then the same procedure should be done to compute that loading, only the depth of the photoload picture fuelbed is assumed to be the highest diameter of the size class. So a slash bed composed of a 10 hour woody fuelbed that is 10 cm deep might be matched with the photoload picture of 5 kg m^{-2} but the actual loading would be the product of the photoload estimated loading (5.0 kg m^{-2}) and the depth of the fuelbed (0.1 meters) divided by largest diameter of the 10 hour class. For example, the 10 hour fuel class goes from 0.6 cm (0.25 inches) to 2.5 cm (1 inch) so the largest diameter is 0.025 meters and the final loading estimate would be 20 kg m^{-2} (5 kg m^{-2} x 0.1 meter deep / 0.025 meter diameter). The proportional height adjustment may be an oversimplification of how to correct for differences in vegetation height and more research is needed to more accurately describe the relationship of height to loading for important plant species.

We also recommend that the final estimate of fuel loading be adjusted to account for the variability of the fuel within the sampling unit. This is done by matching photoload pictures with all levels of fuel loading within the sample unit and then performing a weighted average based on percent area of these loadings with the estimated proportions of the fuel loading levels within the sampling unit. So, if we have a 1000 m^2 plot and found that the ocular estimates for fuel loadings were 0.1 kg m^{-2} for 10 percent of the plot, and 1.1 kg m^{-2} for 50 percent of the plot, and 2.0 kg m^{-2} for 40 percent of the plot, then the final loading would be 1.36 kg m^{-2} [((0.1 kg m^{-2} x 10%) + (1.1 kg m^{-2} x 50%) + (2 kg m^{-2} x 40%)) / 100]. This same concept can be used to adjust for loadings within the 1x1 meter photo frame used in the photoload sequences.

We found that photoload estimations are most accurate when the sampling unit is small (fig. 6 compared with fig. 10). The least bias occurred when the evaluation participants estimated loadings at the microplot level (table 4). However, most applications of the photoload technique may be done at scales much larger than one square meter. Therefore, we have developed a microplot sampling strategy in the photoload sampling protocol that allows the user to implement a nested and stratified random sample of photoload microplots across a large sampling unit to more accurately estimate fuel loadings and to provide the user with a measure of variability. This procedure involves establishing microplots at various distances along transects that bisect a sample unit such as a stand or plot. These transects can be arranged in a way that best fits the sampling objective. We suggest that if accurate loadings are required, then the fixed plot or planar intersect techniques are probably better than the photoload sampling technique. However, if there isn't the time, equipment, or expertise to implement fixed plots or planar intersect methods, then the photoload technique should be employed using the nested microplot strategy provided sufficient time or the macroplot strategy if time is limited. The photo series and photoload sampling techniques can be integrated to achieve higher quality loading estimates.

Log loadings are especially difficult to estimate using the photoload technique because the photoload pictures do not fully portray the diameters of the logs on site. Since log loading increases by the square of the diameter, small changes in log diameter can result in large changes in log loading. Moreover, log decay can also influence loading estimates. We recommend that the photoload user utilize the log loading tables in Keane and Dickinson (2007; RMRS-GTR-190) to calibrate, adjust, and refine the ocular measurements obtained by the photoload sequences. To use these tables, the user simply estimates the average diameter of the logs within a fixed area (we suggest 10 by 10 meters so that it corresponds to the area in the photoload log pictures) and the length of log in the area. These estimates are then referenced in the tables to get the loading. The user can measure log diameters and length with a ruler or tape to get more accurate loading estimates. The integration of this tabular technique with the photoload technique should provide consistent estimates of loadings, especially when the loadings are high. We also suggest that this same process be used to adjust 100 hour woody fuel loading since loadings can vary greatly across the diameter class width (1 to 3 inches or 2.5 to 7.5 cm). Last, estimating log loadings in heavy fuels might be more time-consuming than traditional planar intersect methods, so the photoload technique may be more efficient in natural fuels where down log loadings are light.

Limitations of the photoload sampling technique— The photoload method relies on the ability of the sampler to visually match observed fuel loadings with the loadings portrayed in a series of pictures in the photoload sequences. Fuelbeds observed in the field often contain a mixture of all fuel components and it may be difficult for the sampler to visually single out just one fuel component from the hodgepodge of sticks, leaves, and vegetation on the ground. This is especially true for the fine woody debris because one single stick may be composed of two and maybe three woody fuel size classes. The depth of the woody fuel is also not entirely evident in the fine woody photoload series so it may be difficult to estimate loadings when the particles are randomly arranged in three dimensions (having significant tilt as in nature) rather than neatly arranged in two dimensions as in the photoload sequences. Next, the high variability of wood density (specific gravity) across and within woody fuel components (table 2) can also contribute to photoload estimation errors. For example, the density of the wood in the photoload sequences might not match the density of wood observed in the field by the sampler because of species, fuel age, and environmental differences. It is also difficult to get a full sense of shrub and herb density with the photoload pictures so subtle changes in fuel loadings due to the variability in density contribute to estimation errors. The shrub and herb photoload sequences do not adequately portray the way plants grow in nature in both size and arrangement; plants are usually clustered and are rarely uniform in distribution.

Perhaps the greatest drawback of the photoload technique is that it relies on visual estimations to obtain fuel loading. Visual estimates of loading, much like ocular estimates of vegetation cover, are subject to human error because they rely on subjective assessments with an imperfect measuring device – the eye (Mueller-Dombois and Ellenberg 1974; Bonham 1989). Without a standard or benchmark, it is difficult to describe the error in a visual estimate. Ocular estimates are only somewhat consistent and accurate for a single observer, and often difficult to repeat among different observers. The characteristics of the fuelbed can also influence a person's ocular estimate. Fine woody material, for example, might be easy to estimate on a forest floor of only pine needles but difficult to estimate for a forest floor with substantial shrub cover or log cover. As we found in our accuracy assessment, high fuel loadings contribute to larger errors in ocular estimation because the fuel types are mixed and obscured (figs. 9 and 12). The human eye sometimes has a hard time discriminating among components without extensive practice. We found that the precision of the ocular estimates gets better as experience in photoload fuel sampling increases. Additional testing of this technique is needed as more fuelbeds are photographed and these methods are applied to other ecosystems.

Conclusions

The photoload sampling technique appears to be a viable means of estimating fuel loading for input into fire behavior and effects modeling. It performs quite well under many fuel conditions and the accuracy and precision of the estimates appears to improve with sampling experience. It appears to be a useful means of estimating fuel loadings of common surface fuel components. User's may tend to underestimate actual fuel loadings with the photoload sampling technique, but this can be corrected with abundant calibration exercises and extensive field experience.

References

Agee, J. K. 1993. Fire ecology of Pacific Northwest forests. Washington, DC: Island Press.

Albini, F. A. 1976. Estimating wildfire behavior and effects. Ogden, UT: U.S. Department of Agriculture, Forest Service, Intermountain Research Station. Gen. Tech. Rep. INT-30. 39 p.

Bonham, C. D. 1989. Measurements for terrestrial vegetation. New York: John Wiley & Sons.

Brown, J. K. 1970. A method for inventorying downed woody fuel. Ogden, UT: U.S. Department of Agriculture, Forest Service, Intermountain Research Station. Gen. Tech. Rep. INT-16. 44 p.

Brown, J. K. 1971. A planar intersect method for sampling fuel volume and surface area. Forest Science. 17:96-102.

Brown, J. K. 1974. Handbook for inventorying downed woody material. Ogden, UT: U.S. Department of Agriculture, Forest Service, Intermountain Forest and Range Experiment Station. Gen. Tech. Rep. INT-16. 68 p.

Brown, J. K., R. D. Oberheu, and C. M. Johnston. 1982. Handbook for inventorying surface fuels and biomass in the Interior West. Ogden, UT: U.S. Department of Agriculture, Forest Service, Intermountain Forest and Range Experiment Station. Gen. Tech. Rep. INT-129. 88 p.

Brown, J. K., and C. D. Bevins. 1986. Surface fuel loadings and predicted fire behavior for vegetation types in the northern Rocky Mountains. Ogden, UT: U.S. Department of Agriculture, Forest Service, Intermountain Forest and Range Experiment Station Res. Note INT-358. 25 p.

Brown, J. K., and T. E. See. 1981. Downed dead woody fuel and biomass in the northern Rocky Mountains. Ogden, UT: U.S. Department of Agriculture, Forest Service, Intermountain Forest and Range Experiment Station. Gen. Tech. Rep. INT-117. 33 p.

Burgan, R. E. 1987. Concepts and interpreted examples in advanced fuel modeling. Ogden, UT: U.S. Department of Agriculture, Forest Service, Intermountain Forest and Range Experiment Station. Gen. Tech. Rep. INT-238. 99 p.

Burgan, R. E., and R. C. Rothermel. 1984. BEHAVE: fire behavior prediction and fuel modeling system—FUEL subsystem. Ogden, UT: U.S. Department of Agriculture, Forest Service, Intermountain Research Station. Gen. Tech. Rep. INT-167. 44 p.

DeBano, L. F., D. G. Neary, and P. F. Ffolliott. 1998. Fire's effect on ecosystems. New York: John Wiley & Sons.

Fischer, W. C. 1981. Photo guide for appraising downed woody fuels in Montana forests: Interior ponderosa pine, ponderosa pine-larch-Douglas-fir, larch-Douglas-fir, and Interior Douglas-fir cover types. Ogden, UT: U.S. Department of Agriculture, Forest Service, Intermountain Forest and Range Experiment Station. Gen. Tech. Rep. INT-97. 67 p.

Fosberg, M. A. 1970. Drying rates of heartwood below fiber saturation. Forest Science. 16:57-63.

GAO. 2003. Additional actions required to better identify and prioritize lands needing fuels reduction. Report to Congressional Requesters GAO-03-805. Washington, DC; General Accounting Office.

GAO. 2004. Forest Service and BLM need better information and a systematic approach for assessing risks of environmental effects. GAO-04-705. Washington, DC. General Accounting Office.

Gove, J. H., M. J. Ducey, G. Stahl, and A. Ringvall. 2001. Point relascope sampling: A new way to assess downed coarse woody debris. Journal of Forestry. April:4-11.

Gove, J. H., A. Ringvall, G. Stahl, and M. J. Ducey. 1999. Point relascope sampling of downed coarse woody debris. Canadian Journal of Forest Research. 29:1718-1726.

Harmon, M. E., J. F. Franklin, F. J. Swanson, P. Sollins, S. V. Gregory, J. D. Lattin, N. H. Anderson, S. P. Cline, N. G. Aumen, J. R. Sedell, G. W. Lienkaemper, K. Cromack, and K. W. Cummins. 1986. Ecology of coarse woody debris in temperate ecosystems. Advances in Ecological Research. 15:133-302.

Harmon, M. E., and J. Sexton. 1996. Guidelines for measurement of woody debris in forest ecosystems. Publ. No. 20. U.S. LTER Network, Seattle, WA: University of Washington.

Keane, R. E., R. E. Burgan, and J. V. Wagtendonk. 2001. Mapping wildland fuels for fire management across multiple scales: Integrating remote sensing, GIS, and biophysical modeling. International Journal of Wildland Fire. 10:301-319.

Keane, Robert E., Dickinson, Laura J. 2007. The photoload sampling technique: estimating surface fuel loadings from downward-looking photographs of synthetic fuelbeds. Fort Collins, CO: U.S. Department of Agriculture, Forest Service, Rocky Mountain Research Station. Gen. Tech. Rep. RMRS-GTR-190. 44 p.

Laverty, L., and J. Williams. 2000. Protecting people and sustaining resources in fire-adapted ecosystems—a cohesive strategy. Forest Service response to GAO Report GAO/RCED 99-65. Washington, DC. U.S. Department of Agriculture, Forest Service.

Lutes, D. C. 1999. A comparison of methods for the quantification of coarse woody debris and identification of its spatial scale: a study from the Tenderfoot Experimental Forest, Montana. Missoula, MT: The University of Montana. Thesis. 120 p.

Lutes, D. C. 2002. Assessment of the line transect method: an examination of the spatial patterns. Albany, CA: U.S. Department of Agriculture, Forest Service, Pacific Southwest Research Station. Gen. Tech. Rep. PSW-GTR-181. 13 p.

Lutes, D. C. [In prep]. Predicted fuel consumption in the BURNUP model: sensitivity to four user inputs. Fort Collins, CO: U.S. Department of Agriculture, Forest Service, Rocky Mountain Research Station. Res. Note RMRS-RN-XX.

Lutes, D. C., R. E. Keane, and J. F. Caratti. [In prep]. Fuel Loading Models: A national classification of wildland fuelbeds for fire effects modeling. Canadian Journal of Forest Research.

Lutes, D. C., R. E. Keane, J. F. Caratti, C. H. Key, N. C. Benson, S. Sutherland, and L. J. Gangi. 2006. FIREMON: Fire effects monitoring and inventory system. Fort Collins, CO: U.S. Department of Agriculture, Forest Service, Rocky Mountain Research Station. Gen. Tech. Rep. RMRS-GTR-164CD.

Mueller-Dombois, D., and H. Ellenberg. 1974. Aims and methods of vegetation ecology. New York: John Wiley & Sons.

Mutch, R. W. 1994. A return to ecosystem health. Journal of Forestry. 92:31-33.

Ottmar, R. D., M. F. Burns, J. N. Hall, and A. D. Hanson. 1993. CONSUME users guide. Portland, OR: U.S. Department of Agriculture, Forest Service, Pacific Northwest Research Station. Gen. Tech. Rep. PNW-GTR-304. 44 p.

Ottmar, R. D., R.E. Vihnanek, C. S. Wright, and D. Olsen. 2004. Stereo photo series for quantifying natural fuels. Volume VII: Oregon white oak, California deciduous oak, and mixed conifer with shrub types in the western United States. U.S. Department of Agriculture, Forest Service, National Wildfire Coordinating Group, National Interagency Fire Center. 76 p.

Rauscher, M. H., M. J. Young, and C. D. Webb. 2000. Testing the accuracy of growth and yield models for southern hardwood forests. Southern Journal of Applied Forestry. 24:176-185.

Reinhardt, E., and R. E. Keane. 1998. FOFEM—a First Order Fire Effects Model. Fire Management Notes. 58:25-28.

Reinhardt, E., R.E. Keane, and J. K. Brown. 1997. First Order Fire Effects Model: FOFEM 4.0 User's Guide. Ogden, UT: U.S. Department of Agriculture, Forest Service, Intermountain Research Station. Gen. Tech. Rep. INT-GTR-344. 45 p.

Rothermel, R. C. 1972. A mathematical model for predicting fire spread in wildland fuels. Ogden, UT: U.S. Department of Agriculture, Forest Service, Intermountain Forest and Range Experiment Station Res. Pap. INT-115. 105 p.

Sandberg, D. V., R. D. Ottmar, and G. H. Cushon. 2001. Characterizing fuels in the 21st century. International Journal of Wildland Fire. 10:381-387.

Scott, Joe H. and E. D. Reinhardt. 2005. Stereo photo guide for estimating canopy fuel characteristics in conifer stands. Fort Collins, CO: U.S. Department of Agriculture, Forest Service, Rocky Mountain Research Station. Gen. Tech. Rep. RMRS-GTR-145. 49 p.

Sikkink, P. G. and R. E. Keane. 2008 [in press]. A comparison of five sampling techniques to estimate downed woody fuels in montane forests. International Journal of Wildland Fire.

van Wagner, C. E. 1968. The line intersect method in forest fuel sampling. Forest Science. 14:20-26.

van Wagner, C. E. 1977. Conditions for the start and spread of crown fire. Canadian Journal of Forest Research. 7:23-34.

Van Wagtendonk, J. W., J. M. Benedict, and W. M. Sydoriak. 1996. Physical properties of woody fuel particles of Sierra Nevada conifers. International Journal of Wildland Fire. 6:117-123.

Wenger, K. F. 1984. Forestry Handbook, 2nd Edition. New York: John Wiley & Sons.

www.ingramcontent.com/pod-product-compliance
Lightning Source LLC
Chambersburg PA
CBHW080744290526
45790CB00008B/3315